JOE TOMLINSON

JUSTICE IN THE DIGITAL STATE

Assessing the next revolution in administrative justice

T0324315

POLICY PRESS **SHORTS** POLICY & PRACTICE

First published in Great Britain in 2019 by

Policy Press
University of Bristol
1-9 Old Park Hill
Bristol
BS2 8BB
UK
t: +44 (0)117 954 5940
pp-info@bristol.ac.uk
www.policypress.co.

North America office:
Policy Press
c/o The University of Chicago Press
1427 East 60th Street
Chicago, IL 60637, USA
t: +1 773 702 7700
f: +1 773 702 9756
sales@press.uchicago.edu
www.press.uchicago.edu

British Library Cataloguing in Publication Data
A catalogue record for this book is available from the British Library.

Library of Congress Cataloging-in-Publication Data
A catalog record for this book has been requested.

ISBN 978-1-4473-4017-1 (paperback)
ISBN 978-1-4473-4018-8 (ePub)
ISBN 978-1-4473-4029-4 (Mobi)
ISBN 978-1-4473-4033-1 (OA PDF)

Cover design by Policy Press
Front cover: image kindly supplied by istock
Printed and bound in Great Britain by CMP, Poole
Policy Press uses environmentally responsible print partners

For Elizabeth

Contents

Acknowledgements

The impetus for writing this book came from being in various rooms where those concerned with public law and administrative justice – working in research, legal practice, policy-making, the charity sector and other vocations – were gradually reckoning with the impact of technology on their sphere of activity. There have long been lawyers with a specialist interest in technology, but now it is all public lawyers who are having to pay attention to technology's diverse impacts. Such changes can, especially for those operating at the coalface, be difficult to make sense of in a wider context. Yet a wider understanding is an essential part of formulating appropriate responses to these developments. My hope is that this short book will provide a framework that assists and encourages readers to do that sort of thinking about the challenges and opportunities that technology presents for the administrative justice system.

In writing this book, I have incurred numerous debts of gratitude. Dr Richard Kirkham gave very detailed and helpful comments on Chapter One. He also encouraged me to take up the task of writing this book in the first place. I presented some of the ideas in Chapter One at a conference on administrative justice in Wales organised by Dr Sarah Nason, where participants gave many helpful comments. Chapter Two has been a focus area of my research in the past few years. I have presented ideas on crowdfunded judicial reviews at both the University of Oxford and the University of Essex, where input from attendees helped me to develop my thinking. I am particularly grateful to Professor Maurice Sunkin for comments at various events and on various draft papers, which always gave me cause to think further. Chapter Three builds on research that I have been doing with various people in recent years, in particular with Professor Robert Thomas and Byron Karemba. I presented the ideas that form the basis of Chapter Three at the Melbourne Public Law Conference in the summer of 2018. Chapter Four benefited from a variety of discussions, including with the dedicated civil servants working on various ongoing reform projects. A visiting position at Osgoode Hall Law School in 2017, which was kindly supported by Professor Lorne Sossin (now Justice Sossin), allowed me to engage with the Winkler Institute on some of these issues, as well as others in Toronto interested in the field of legal design. Toronto provided the space to develop much of the research presented in Chapter Four.

I have benefited greatly from many discussions on the topic of digitalisation generally, including with Professor Robert Thomas, Professor Carol Harlow, Professor Roger Smith, Caroline Sheppard, Sara Lomri, Professor Michael Adler, Dr Jen Raso, Dr Kristen Rundle, Dr Abi Adams, Dr Jeremias Prassl, Margaret Doyle, Dr Natalie Byrom and Matthew Ahluwalia. Dr Adam Harkens provided excellent research assistance on various parts of the book. The UK Administrative Justice Institute and the Administrative Justice Council also provided lively forums to discuss ideas relating to digitalisation.

A particular note of thanks is reserved for the exceptional team at the Public Law Project, an organisation where I have been fortunate enough to serve as Research Director since 2017. The team at the Public Law Project is an incredibly reflective and creative group of practitioners and researchers. Working with them has forced me to rethink some of my assumptions (which may have otherwise been left intact within the walls of an academic institution). Seeing them grapple with the unfolding HM Courts & Tribunals Service (HMCTS) reform project, and various other technological developments within the public law system, was a key part of the motivation for writing this book. All views expressed here are mine and do not represent the policy of the Public Law Project.

The team at Bristol University Press – particularly Helen Davis, Rebecca Tomlinson and Christie Smith – have been fantastic to work with in the production of this book. They understood and supported the purpose of the book from the outset.

Finally, I must record a sincere thanks to my family and friends for putting up with me for the long periods I have had my head in my books and laptop while researching public law, administrative justice and digitalisation. A particular thanks goes to my partner, Elizabeth, who not only puts up with me, but also encourages me every day.

Preface

Administrative justice – the processes through which the state makes decisions about people and the avenues by which they can challenge those decisions – is increasingly affected by technology. Early attempts at 'E-government' now appear to be accelerating at speed towards the full emergence of the digital administrative state. This short book examines three very different ways in which the UK's administrative justice system is changing due to the influence of technology: the increase in crowdfunded judicial reviews; the digitalisation of tribunals; and the adoption of 'agile' methodologies by civil servants tasked with building the administrative justice system. Taking a functional approach, this book sets out a framework for understanding and analysing the varied impacts of new technology on administrative justice, revolving around four central issues: evidence, politics, models and design. It argues that, while the growing role of technology should not make us lose sight of the fact that the essential character of government will remain a social, human endeavour, ensuring justice in the digital state is a task that requires us to both study closely the empirical consequences of technology and revisit, and maybe even abandon, existing frameworks for understanding how administrative justice operates.

Foreword

Carol Harlow

E-government has been with us for many years – since the early 1990s in fact – although at first only in the sense of technical assistance with repetitive tasks, such as filing cabinets leaving the office floor and going online, email replacing the post, and so on. This was hardly challenging. The first experiments with algorithmic risk assessment, video-linked evidence in court and telephonic legal advice that followed were readily accepted by lawyers while the arrival of parking adjudicators, the first online hearings in this country, went virtually unnoticed. Recently, however, the pace of change has accelerated sharply, impinging more on legal processes. While the administrative assistant is taking on the role of sorcerer's apprentice who, with his robotic friends, is colonising the legal world, we, like the sorcerer, have mostly been sleeping.

Joe Tomlinson, however, has joined the handful of pioneering lawyers who have set out to question, evaluate and explain the new developments. He has drawn attention at academic seminars and conferences to the changes that are occurring in the area of administrative justice that is his particular specialism, and the potential problems they may throw up. He has worked with the Public Law Project to get together empirical evidence of what is going on. He has used the new technology to publicise the issues by posting blogs and subscribing to online hubs and networks. This new book takes his work a stage further. By bringing together earlier case studies on which he has been working, he conveys a warning about changes to the system as a whole.

The first case study concerns the funding of judicial review, made perilous by savage cuts to legal aid. Tomlinson looks at crowdfunding as a possible answer, and the arrival on the scene of commercial and political platforms, with the possible effects on public interest litigation as the impending model of judicial review. Given that crowdfunding is still in its infancy, Tomlinson is right to be tentative in his conclusions. While it has helped support cases that would not have otherwise been brought, crowdfunding has the potential to disrupt 'relatively stable patterns and practices of public interest judicial review litigation.' So watch this space carefully.

In the area of tribunals, where digitalisation is proceeding alongside a steady closing down of real tribunals and courts, access to justice is a major issue. The government maintains that online processes will increase access to justice for the many; in the light of the experience with Universal Credit, those who work with applicants for social security benefits are less sure. Tomlinson calls the reforms 'a major policy gamble by a government under pressure to reduce costs.' Linking digitalisation with the trend to replace tribunal hearings with internal, mandatory review, Tomlinson argues that any online appeal system must be 'designed to fit into the wider administrative justice landscape', raising the question, how is digital justice being adopted, designed and made?

Tomlinson provides a simple introduction to the world of 'agile' and 'design thinking' approaches that dominate the thinking of the Government Digital Service and have infiltrated government policy-making in recent years. On the credit side, 'agile processes' place 'a greater emphasis on evidence-based policy-making'; they can be more open and participatory, allowing the actual voices of users to be heard. Keeping an open mind on a practice that is clearly in its infancy, Tomlinson confines himself to recommending that greater space must be made for 'wider concerns of ethics and good governance' within the design-thinking mindset and the 'agile processes' by which it is carried through.

Under the influence of American thinking and notably the pioneering work of Jerry Mashaw (*Bureaucratic Justice; Managing Social Security Claims*, Yale University Press, 1983), administrative justice itself has travelled a long way in a relatively short time – from a handful of High Court actions to an Administrative Court, from a random assortment of tribunals to tribunals as equal partners with the civil courts, from courts and tribunals to at least the conception of an inclusive and 'proportionate' set of processes for dispute resolution. Technology will, by and large, facilitate the journey to redress. On the way, a set of core values has been built into administrative justice: openness, fairness and impartiality; accountability, transparency and participation; the right to a hearing and other due process values; and access to justice as a constitutional right. These are hard-won values that we must be careful not to compromise. I am therefore grateful to Joe Tomlinson for providing a framework which assists and encourages readers to do that sort of thinking about the challenges and opportunities that technology presents for the administrative justice system. I hope that his short and accessible book will be widely read and discussed.

Carol Harlow is Emerita Professor of Law at the London School of Economics and Political Science

List of abbreviations

DWP	Department for Work and Pensions
ESA	Employment and Support Allowance
FtTIAC	First-tier Tribunal (Immigration and Asylum) Chamber
HMCTS	Her Majesty's Courts & Tribunals Service
MoJ	Ministry of Justice
MR	Mandatory reconsideration
NGO	Non-governmental organisation
PIP	Personal Independence Payment
SSCS	Social Security and Child Support Tribunal
UN	United Nations

ONE

A functional framework

The administrative justice system is the mechanism through which government makes decisions about citizens' rights and entitlements (in respect of, for example, social security, immigration and housing), and the processes through which people can challenge those decisions (for example, through judicial review, ombuds and tribunals).[1] By scale, administration is by far the largest part of the state: it is where high-level policy discussions transform into the street-level coercion of citizens.[2] Like many other areas of law, society and government, administrative justice is now beginning to see the impacts of rapid technological advances. Early attempts at 'E-government'

---

[1] Administrative justice is also considered to be an aspect of the public and administrative law systems. I use the terms flexibly here. For a recent overview of the dynamics within administrative justice, see Thomas, Robert and Tomlinson, Joe (2017) 'Mapping current issues in administrative justice: Austerity and the "more bureaucratic rationality" approach', *Journal of Social Welfare and Family Law*, 39(3), 380.

[2] Zacka, Bernardo (2017) *Where the State Meets the Street: Public Service and Moral Agency*, Cambridge, MA: Harvard University Press.

and using 'ICT'[3] are now accelerating towards the emergence of the digital administrative state, and the prophecies of futurologists are being put to the test.[4] The essential promise of technology remains, as it always has done, of more and better for less effort.[5] The fundamental concern also remains the same; that by using new technology, we alienate older methods – and their benefits – that we ought to be preserving.[6] Looking at the present situation surrounding the developing digitalisation of administrative justice, it is clear that some new political dynamics are emerging as a result of recent changes. Activists are using online crowdfunding platforms to fund challenges to the policies of the government in the courts, advancing their campaigns through social media.[7] At the same time, a Conservative government – pursuing a long-term programme of fiscal austerity in response to the global financial crisis of 2008 – is attempting the most ambitious digitalisation of courts

---

[3] See, for example, Margetts, Helen and Partington, Martin (2010) 'Developments in E-government', in Michael Adler (ed) *Administrative Justice in Context*, Oxford: Hart Publishing, Chapter 3; Bovens, Mark and Zouridis, Stavros (2002) 'From Street-level to System-level Bureaucracies: How Information and Communication Technology Is Transforming Administrative Discretion and Constitutional Control', *Public Administration Review*, 62(2), 174–84.

[4] Susskind, Richard (2017) *Tomorrow's Lawyers: An Introduction to Your Future* (2nd edn), Oxford: Oxford University Press.

[5] Similar basic claims made about technology were seen during the Industrial Revolution; see, for example, Daunton, Martin (1995) *Progress and Poverty: An Economic and Social History of Britain 1700–1850*, Oxford: Oxford University Press.

[6] Ibid.

[7] For instance, there has been a string of crowdfunded claims (of variable merit) seeking to challenge the government's approach to Brexit, such as *R (Webster) v Secretary of State for Exiting the EU* [2018] EWHC 1543 (Admin); *R (Miller) v Secretary of State for Exiting the European Union* [2017] UKSC 5.

and tribunals ever seen.[8] The gamble is that slashing the justice budget, cutting approximately 5,000 court staff and closing hearing centres will not undermine but improve access to justice *if* the promise of technology is realised.[9] These examples merely scratch the surface of how digitalisation is starting to change the workings of administrative justice.

How are we to make sense of the present situation and the changes ahead? This is a core question facing many of those concerned with the administrative justice system in the UK: policy-makers, civil servants, non-governmental organisations (NGOs), judges, lawyers, researchers, citizens and others. This is also a puzzle for international observers, who are seeing – or will likely soon see – the impacts of technology on administrative justice in their own jurisdictions. In this book I set out a framework – based on four central issues – for understanding and analysing the varied impacts of new technology on administrative justice. I then apply this framework in the context of three case studies in each of the subsequent chapters. In selecting the case studies included here, my aim is not to be comprehensive, but to consider a wide range of technology-linked changes to administrative justice processes in the UK.[10] The case studies

---

[8] These reforms are discussed in detail in Chapter Three. For general context, *see* Rozenberg, Joshua (2018) *The Online Court: Will IT Work?*, Guildford: Legal Education Foundation; Thomas, Robert and Tomlinson, Joe (2018) 'Remodelling social security appeals (again): The advent of online tribunals', *Journal of Social Security Law*, 25(2), 84–101.

[9] Ministry of Justice (2016) *Transforming Our Justice System*, London. For a recent overview, see National Audit Office (2018) *Early Progress in Transforming Courts and Tribunals*, HC 1001, Session 2017–2019; House of Commons Committee of Public Accounts (2018) *Transforming Courts and Tribunals*, HC 976.

[10] There are thus lots of areas I do not cover here which require detailed study. One important area is administrative decision-making; see, for example, Eubanks, Virginia (2018) *Automating Inequality: How High-tech Tools Profile, Police, and Punish the Poor*, New York: St Martin's Press; Oswald, Marion (2018) 'Algorithm-assisted decision-making in the public sector:

cover instances of the effects of technology both in internal government processes as well as external justice processes, such as courts and tribunals. They examine examples of changes imposed as part of public service provision and also where technology has led to change from the ground up. Some of the studies concern 'hard' process changes involving technology, whereas others look at the 'soft' cultural influence of technology and its associated modes of thought.

In Chapter Two I examine the growing use of crowdfunding – raising money via online platforms – as a means of covering the costs of judicial review cases. In Chapter Three I look at the ongoing HM Courts & Tribunals Service (HMCTS) 'transformation' project, which is putting courts and tribunals on a digital footing. My particular focus in that chapter is on the digitalisation of tribunals, where individuals can appeal government decisions. In the final chapter, I consider the use of new 'agile' methodologies – adopted and promoted by the technology industry and subsequently, civil servants – in building administrative justice systems. All of these issues throw up complex questions but, as has increasingly been recognised in recent years, the need for analysis in this quickly changing aspect of the administrative justice landscape is becoming more urgent, and so far, such analysis has been relatively scarce.

The approach adopted and advocated for in this book is a functionalist one.[11] My operating assumption is that the administrative justice system is ultimately social in character, as

---

Framing the issues using administrative law rules governing discretionary power', *Philosophical Transactions of the Royal Society A*, 376, 2128.

[11] For a detailed account of the foundations of this approach, see Loughlin, Martin (2005) 'The functionalist style in public law', *University of Toronto Law Journal*, 55, 361–403; Loughlin, Martin (2014) 'Modernism in British public law, 1919–1979', *Public Law*, 56. This is not an uncontested approach; for context, see Loughlin, Martin (1992) *Public Law and Political Theory*, Oxford: Clarendon Press. Nor, too, is the identification of functionalism a distinct approach; see, for example, Craig, Paul (2015) *UK,*

it still fundamentally revolves around the collectivist activities carried out by the state. Given this, my view is that administrative justice ought to evolve with society and be part of promoting a healthy *body politic*, focusing not just on controlling state power but enabling it too. I adopt the outlook that it is important to study all aspects of the relationship between law and administration – including the approach of administrators and all systems of redress – and not just the law as it is discussed by judges in courts. From this starting point, I suggest it is helpful to keep in mind four interrelated central issues that anyone seeking to understand the digitalisation of administrative justice must grapple with. These issues, which have long been core concerns of the administrative justice community, are evidence, politics, models and design. I will now elaborate each aspect of this framework in more detail.

Evidence

Digitalisation presents a set of new developments, and the primary task at the outset must be to understand the nature and impacts of these developments. Does the introduction of online social security appeals lead to more or less people being in receipt of benefits? Does the use of crowdfunding lead to more judicial reviews claims being lodged? Discussion about administrative justice has often suffered from a deficient evidence base. If we are to make claims about what systems ought to look like, facts are highly relevant. This may seem obvious, but public law research in the UK has failed regularly in this most fundamental of descriptive tasks in recent years. Although there are some noteworthy exceptions,[12] the priority of the

---

EU and Global Administrative Law: Foundations and Challenges, Cambridge: Cambridge University Press, p 103 *et seq.*

[12] For instance, Maurice Sunkin has made a significant contribution to the understanding of how the judicial review system works in practice; see, for

majority of public law research – in line with prevailing academic trends[13] – is to try to identify 'the patterns, continuities, and discontinuities thinking displays, and the manner in which it shapes the politically possible.'[14] As a result, the field of public law is now heavy on insight and light on descriptive accounts of what is actually happening within the system.[15]

One consequence of this situation is that important debates about the desired outcomes that systems ought to achieve, or how systems ought to be designed, are complicated or obscured by lack of knowledge about (often relatively basic) facts.[16]

---

example, Sunkin, Maurice, Calvo, Kerman, Platt, Lucinda and Landman, Todd (2007) 'Mapping the use of judicial review to challenge local authorities in England and Wales', *Public Law*, 545–67; Sunkin, Maurice and Bondy, Varda (2008) 'Accessing judicial review', *Public Law*, 647; Sunkin, Maurice and Bondy, Varda (2009) 'Settlement in judicial review proceedings', *Public Law*, 237–59; Bondy, Varda, Platt, Lucinda and Sunkin, Maurice (2015) *The Value and Effects of Judicial Review: The Nature of Claims, their Outcomes and Consequences*, London: Public Law Project. For a wider context, see Halliday, Simon (2012) 'Public Law', in C. Hunter (ed) *Integrating Socio-Legal Studies into the Law Curriculum*, Basingstoke: Palgrave Macmillan, pp 141–60.

[13] These trends are well traced in Tschorne Venegas, Samuel (2016) 'The theoretical turn in British public law scholarship', PhD thesis, London: London School of Economics and Political Science.

[14] Freeden, Michael (1996) *Ideologies and Political Theory*, Oxford: Clarendon Press, p 39; Freeden, Michael (2000) 'Practising ideology and ideological practices', *Political Studies*, 48, 302–22, p 304.

[15] Those interested in understanding the details of systems have commonly delved into to sub-fields such as social security law, immigration law, tax law and regulation; see, for example, Thomas, Robert (2011) *Administrative Justice and Asylum Appeals: A Study of Tribunal Adjudication*, Oxford: Hart Publishing.

[16] A very good example of this is the debate around how costs in judicial review cases are distributed. Lord Justice Jackson undertook a detailed review over a number of years, yet the absence of data (particularly quantitative data) in the review was remarkable; see Lord Justice Jackson (2009) *Review of Civil Litigation Costs: Final Report*; Lord Justice Jackson (2017) *Review of Civil Litigation Costs: Supplemental Report, Fixed Recoverable Costs*.

This situation could have often been avoided – or its impact could at least have been mitigated – if there was more focus in public law research on building descriptive accounts of how the administrative justice system works. This neglect of evidence-gathering can also be linked, at least in part, to the fact that administrative justice policy and system design has remained largely in the grip of professional judgement (mostly that of lawyers and civil servants) instead of moving towards greater reliance on evidence.[17] Whereas medicine has been able to transform itself into a primarily evidence-based science in the last century,[18] public law research – and law more generally – has largely resisted following a similar trajectory.[19]

In recent years, there have been some attempts by public lawyers, often with political science and social science backgrounds, to undertake empirical research on a range of important public law questions; for example, do constitutionally entrenched fundamental rights generally deliver on their promise of protecting people from harm and promoting social welfare?[20]

Researchers undertaking these studies are coming under increasing fire for a variety of reasons, often because of concerns about the links between cause and effects being drawn and

---

[17] For a general discussion, see Greiner, D. James and Matthews, Andrea (2016) 'Randomized control trials in the United States legal profession', *Annual Review of Law and Social Science*, 12, 295–312.

[18] Meldrum, Marcia L. (2000) 'A brief history of the randomized control trial: From oranges and lemons to the Gold Standard', *Hematology/Oncology Clinics of North America*, 14(4), 745–60.

[19] See Greiner and Matthews (note 17 above).

[20] See, for example, Law, David S. and Versteeg, Mila (2013) 'Sham constitutions', *California Law Review*, 101(4), 863–952; Chilton, Adam S. and Versteeg, Mila (2016) 'Do constitutional rights make a difference?', *American Journal of Political Science*, 60, 561–81, p 575; Chilton, Adam S. and Versteeg, Mila (2018) 'Rights without resources: The impact of constitutional social rights on social spending', *The Journal of Law and Economics*, 60(4),713–48.

a perceived failure to properly contextualise claims.[21] Such critiques may have some validity in particular instances. However, there are many basic questions about administrative justice where concrete data could be gathered and where such data could have great practical utility.[22] For instance, why are successful appeals from immigration decisions successful? This is a basic and fundamental question of administrative justice for which evidence could be found but a question about which there is little clear, systematic evidence available at present.

Evidence will not give us complete answers about administrative justice – we cannot hope to measure our way out of making value judgements – but a better evidence base can provide a firmer platform on which to judge how best to pursue aims. In a recent speech, the Senior President of Tribunals, Sir Ernest Ryder, explained that digitalisation and other reforms are required to enable the judiciary to secure the effective administration of justice. However, the Senior President noted that future reforms can no longer be predicated on the views of a single judge formed on the basis of anecdote or impression: 'reform must be based on proper research; robust and tested.'[23] He concluded: '[i]f we are to secure open justice, all questions must be capable of being asked and examined. But examined properly. The judiciary must therefore support, promote, and commission research. Just as the unexamined life is one not worth living; the unexamined and unresearched reform may not be worth taking.'

It is a recurring theme of this book that there is insufficient evidence available to properly address the questions that the digitalisation of administrative justice presents, even at this

---

[21] Woods, Andrew Keane (2008) 'Discounting rights', *New York University Journal of International Law and Politics*, 50, 509.

[22] Certain processes can also be studied in detail with great success; see, for example, Thomas (note 15 above).

[23] Sir Ernest Ryder (2018) *Securing Open Justice*, Max Planck Institute Luxembourg.

relatively early stage of developments in the digitalisation of administrative justice. As such, further empirical research and data collection will be a vital tool in this area in the future. Empirical research and nuanced data collection could enable better understanding, better learning, better design and continuous improvement. It can analyse and validate the implementation of reforms by providing robust insights into how they are operating. Understanding digitalisation will require the use of a range of empirical methodologies and, moreover, would be enhanced by the pursuit of further methodological innovation.[24] For now, informed accounts on the evidence that is available is the best that can be hoped for.

Politics

A second key aspect of understanding and analysing digitalisation is reckoning with, what we may broadly call, the politics surrounding it. It has long been recognised[25] that administrative justice systems are, to some extent, artefacts of political beliefs: '[b]ehind every theory of administrative law there lies a theory of the state.'[26] These systems – which include both the law and the mechanisms that give practical effect to it – are, at foundational level, instruments through which political objectives can be achieved.[27] We also cannot escape the role of political judgement in assessing them. By using the terms 'politics' I do not hope

---

[24] In particular, under-used methods such as randomised control trials could be explored further in the context of online procedures; see Greiner and Matthews (note 17 above).

[25] See, for example, Laski, Harold (1925) *A Grammar of Politics*, Sydney, NSW: Allen & Unwin, p 578; Carr, Cecil (1941) *Concerning English Administrative Law*, Oxford: Oxford University Press, pp 10–11.

[26] Harlow, Carol and Rawlings, Richard (2009) *Law and Administration* (3rd edn), Cambridge: Cambridge University Press, Chapter 1, p 1.

[27] Duguit, Leon (1921) *Law in the Modern State* (translated by Frida Laski and Harold Laski), Sydney, NSW: Allen & Unwin.

to conjure up the image of something nefarious or unhelpfully partisan (although the tone of present public discourse on politics may create that assumption).[28] Instead, I mean simply a position on the desired outcomes a society and government ought to pursue. In this sense, accounts of whether changes linked to digitalisation are a success or not will ultimately be framed by political judgements of various kinds.

To be clear, politics exists in many variations and all politics can be relevant to the assessment of administrative justice. There is the obvious, broad left–right divide, as well as the myriad positions concealed within that simplistic categorisation. There are also particular politics that emerge around specific policy issues. For instance, the politics of technology, the politics of judicial review and the politics of the legal professions are all highly relevant to some of the issues discussed in this book. There is also a distinct politics of 'good administration' – that is, political views on the extent to which good government itself ought to be prioritised and promoted.[29] Even claims about commitment to the Rule of Law are imbued, or can be associated, with political preferences of some kind.[30]

All politics – whether they are the politics of those in public office or private citizens – are relevant insofar as they provide both the conditions in which developments in the digitalisation of administrative justice will take place and inform the metrics by which those developments can and will be assessed by reference

---

[28] Flinders, Matthew (2012) *Defending Politics*, Oxford: Oxford University Press.

[29] See, for instance, the discussion on the politics of administrative justice oversight in O'Brien, Nick (2012) 'Administrative justice: A libertarian Cinderella in search of an egalitarian prince', *The Political Quarterly*, 83(3), 494–501; O'Brien, Nick (2018) 'Administrative justice in the wake of I, Daniel Blake', *The Political Quarterly*, 89(1), 82–91.

[30] See, for example, Bingham, Tom (2011) *The Rule of Law*, Harmondsworth: Penguin, which is orientated towards a liberal, internationalist conception of the state.

to. In my analysis, presented in the next three chapters of this book, it will inevitably be the case that certain preferences will be advanced and defended. To be able to assess the digitalisation of administrative justice, we must be prepared to understand and confront differing political assessments of various elements of digitalisation.

Models

To understand the digitalisation of administrative justice we must also think closely about the concepts that we commonly rely on when discussing the system. In December 1998, Martin Partington, a central figure in the development of the modern study of administrative justice, gave a lecture on the topic of 'Restructuring administrative justice' at University College London.[31] There, he outlined some of the key concepts of administrative justice: openness, confidentiality, transparency, secrecy, fairness, efficiency, accountability, consistency, participation, rationality, equity and equal treatment. There has been no shortage of other attempts to state the key concepts – often also described as 'principles' or 'values' – that an administrative justice system ought to respect. Indeed, it was observed by the Administrative Justice and Tribunals Council that the UK has a rich history of developing principles for administrative justice.[32] Many such attempts have come from institutions that engage with and are (or were) part of the administrative justice system itself.[33] Academic work also often

---

[31] Partington, Martin (1999) 'Restructuring administrative justice? The redress of citizens' grievances', *Current Legal Problems*, 52(1), 173–99.

[32] Administrative Justice and Tribunals Council (2010) *Developing Principles of Administrative Justice*.

[33] See, for example, Health Service Ombudsman (2009) *Principles of Good Administration*; Administrative Justice and Tribunals Council (2010) *Principles of Administrative Justice*.

refers to a range of similar concepts.[34] Beyond the concepts often specifically associated with administrative justice, the system – including digitalisation – can be considered through a range of other conceptual frameworks. It is now common, for instance, to see human rights analysis of administrative justice processes. Another common frame is that of constitutional principles (for example, the Rule of Law, the separation of powers, democracy, accountability).[35] Discrimination is also a prominent frame in digitalisation research and discussion so far.[36] Civil servants often refer to a particular bundle of concepts too, which often relate to operational concerns, for example, efficiency, proportionate use of resources and manageability.[37] The difficulty is not, therefore, in suggesting concepts that may be relevant to the digitalisation of administrative justice, but in making sense of what to do with all the concepts that are often thrown around.

There are two basic tasks such concepts can be used for: describing the system and assessing the system. When used for the latter purpose (they are often described as 'principles' or 'values' when used to this end), concepts are no more than political claims articulated in another form.[38] When used in this way, concepts can yield important insights. Talking in such terms can also provoke us to reflect closely on the judgements we

---

[34] See, for example, Mashaw, Jerry L. (1985) *Bureaucratic Justice: Managing Social Security Disability Claims*, New Haven, CT: Yale University Press; Adler, Michael (2003) 'A socio-legal approach to administrative justice', *Law & Policy*, 25(4), 323–52.

[35] On the rise of this framework in recent years, see Gee, Graham and Webber, Grégoire (2013) 'Rationalism in public law', *Modern Law Review*, 76(4), 708–34.

[36] See, for example, Gangadharan, Seeta Pena and Jędrzej, Niklas (2018) *Between Antidiscrimination and Data: Understanding Human Rights Discourse on Automated Discrimination in Europe*, London: London School of Economics and Political Science.

[37] Thomas and Tomlinson (note 8 above), referring to the 'government' view on administrative justice.

[38] See Loughlin (2005) (note 11 above).

make.[39] But such concepts have no objective meaning beyond the politics that animate them and the meaning ascribed to them by society. When used for explanatory purposes, concepts can be particularly helpful (in this context they are often referred to as 'models'). Models can help us clarify how systems work, how they are changing, and draw useful distinctions.[40] For instance, Jerry Mashaw's models of administrative justice have, along with subsequent iterations of those models by scholars such as Michael Adler, provided a framework that has enabled generations of observers to understand significant process changes.[41]

Although conceptual frameworks of various types can be valuable, we should take care not to become too bound up in concepts at the expense of how administrative justice actually functions in practice, which should always be the primary consideration.[42] We should also be careful to ensure that reliance on a variety of concepts, especially when hazily defined, does not lead to fuzzy thinking – which has sometimes been the case.[43]

A key point about explanatory concepts made in this book is that, just as the growth of the administrative state and globalisation in the 20th century gave us cause to revisit the concepts through which we understood the state, the growing

---

[39] Nason, Sarah (2016) *Reconstructing Judicial Review*, Oxford: Hart Publishing.

[40] See, for example, Rawlings, Richard (2008) 'Modelling judicial review', *Current Legal Problems*, 61(1), 95–123, p 103.

[41] Mashaw (note 34 above); Adler (note 34 above). See also Richards, Zach (2018) *Responsive Legality: The New Administrative Justice*, Abingdon: Routledge; Kagan, Robert A. (2012) 'The Organisation of Administrative Justice Systems: The Role of Political Mistrust', in Michael Adler (ed) *Administrative Justice in Context*, Oxford: Hart Publishing, Chapter 7; Halliday, Simon and Scott, Colin (2012) 'A Cultural Analysis of Administrative Justice', in Michael Adler (ed) *Administrative Justice in Context*, Oxford: Hart Publishing, Chapter 8.

[42] See Duguit (note 27 above).

[43] Tomlinson, Joe, 'The Grammar of Administrative Justice Values' 39(4) *Journal of Social Welfare and Family Law* 524.

digitalisation of administrative justice gives us cause to do so again.[44] The alternative is to try to understand an increasingly digitalised state by seeking to awkwardly fit developments into possibly outdated frameworks, something that would risk making those who do so pedlars of an increasingly irrelevant nostalgia.[45] Where necessary, we should be willing to reconceptualise and even abandon conventional models of understanding, and devise new models so that we can better explain the changing administrative justice system. At the same time, traditional models may prove important in understanding wrong turns in digitalisation. This is a complex and constantly evolving task, but it is a critical one.

Design

Administrative justice systems give rise to myriad questions of institutional design.[46] For instance, how is the aim of having an

---

[44] For instance, see Rubin, Edward (2005) *Beyond Camelot: Rethinking Politics and Law for the Modern State*, Princeton, NJ: Princeton University Press.

[45] See Rubin, ibid, p 6. The infamous example of this in English administrative law is A.V. Dicey's rejection of the existence of administrative law in England and Wales: Dicey, Albert Venn (1959) *Introduction to the Study of the Law of the Constitution* (10th edn), Basingstoke: Macmillan, pp 336–8. He later had to abandon this position (at least partially) in the face of overwhelming evidence to the contrary: see Dicey, Albert Venn (1915) 'The development of administrative law in England', *Law Quarterly Review*, 31, 148. See also the critique of Maurice Hauriou and Henri Berthélemy in Duguit (note 27 above).

[46] By institutions I mean 'the structures that are to house and refine our disputes and the processes that are to regulate the way we resolve them', a definition taken from Waldron, Jeremy (2013) '*Political* political theory: An inaugural lecture', *Journal of Political Philosophy*, 21(1), p 8. On institutional design in administrative justice in the UK context, see Bondy, Varda and Le Sueur, Andrew (2012) *Designing Redress: A Study About Grievances against Public Bodies*, London: Public Law Project; Tomlinson, Joe and Lovdahl Gormsen, Liza (2018) 'Stumbling towards the UK's new administrative settlement: A study of competition law enforcement after Brexit', *Cambridge Yearbook of*

easy-to-access online tribunal appeal form realised? What should the costs rules applicable to crowdfunded judicial reviews be? How can perceptions of judicial independence be maintained in video-linked hearing processes? Digitalisation presents many such design questions. In one sense, the design of public institutions is the bread and butter of what public lawyers do and are interested in.[47] The actual task of designing public institutions is, however, notoriously difficult. Moreover, the administrative justice system is, to borrow the phrasing of Richard Stewart, densely complex.[48] In this context, designing (or reforming) administrative justice systems is a task riddled with unresolvable tensions and trade-offs. Gunther Teubner argues that these systems are placed under the competing demands of efficacy, responsiveness and coherence.[49] That is to say, citizens and others demand administrative bodies to be successful in managing their role, to be responsive to the public will and to be aligned with the foundational commitments of society. Teubner contends that any design or re-design of an administrative institution that sought to improve its performance in one of these three respects would almost certainly have negative effects on at least one of the other two. In other words, 'from one or another perspective,

---

European Legal Studies, 20, 233–51. For a US perspective, see Mashaw, Jerry, L. (2005) 'Structuring a dense complexity: Accountability and the project of administrative law', *Issues in Legal Scholarship*, 5(1).

[47] For example, Madison, James (1987) 'Federalist No 51', in James Madison, Alexander Hamilton and John Jay (eds) *The Federalist papers*, Harmondsworth: Penguin, p 319. More recently, there have been wide-ranging discussion on constitutional design; see, for example, Ginsburg, Tom (ed) (2012) *Comparative Constitutional Design*, Cambridge: Cambridge University Press.

[48] Stewart, Richard B. (1975) 'The reformation of American administrative law', *Harvard Law* Review, 88, 1667, p 1813.

[49] Teubner, Gunther (1987) 'Juridification: Concepts, aspects, limits, solutions', in Gunther Teubner (ed) *Juridification of Social Spheres: A Comparative Analysis in the Areas of Labor, Corporate, Antitrust, and Social Welfare Law*, Berlin: Walter de Gruyter, 3–48.

every institution will fail, or be seen as partially failing.'[50] In this light, the pursuit of administrative justice could be seen as a 'perpetually unsatisfactory project of institutional design', which even has 'a certain fatalistic hue.'[51] While institutional design is no easy task, it remains at the unavoidable core of administrative justice.

In respect of digitalisation in particular, the approach advocated for in this book is that control of institutional design questions ought not to be yielded to those who possess technological expertise. There is a risk of this in discussions around digitalisation because new technology can be difficult to understand, and it comes with its own (often hidden) methods and politics when deployed in institutions.[52] The social, human project of government is still the essential nature of the administrative justice project and the increasing use of technology should not make us lose sight of this.[53] Moreover, at least for the foreseeable future, humans will still be operating digital systems, and they will certainly be designing them.[54] Technologists have no special authority to make claims about institutional design beyond purely technological solutions. Technology is best conceived as a new material that has been discovered, which is to be added to the existing materials used in building systems. We should understand it as a means for advancing the functions of the state, not as some sort of transcendental change. In this sense, the digitalisation of administrative justice is similar to the expanding

---

[50] See Mashaw (note 34), p 14.

[51] Ibid.

[52] For a discussion, see Mulligan, Deirdre K. and Bamberger, Kenneth A. (2018) 'Saving governance-by-design', *California Law Review*, 106(3).

[53] See, generally, Broad, Ellen (2018) *Made by Humans: The AI Condition*, Melbourne, VIC: Melbourne University Press.

[54] On this aspect of digitalisation, see Raso, Jennifer (2017) 'Displacement as regulation: New regulatory technologies and front-line decision-making in Ontario works', *Canadian Journal of Law and Society*, 32(1), 75–95, p 75.

use of contracted-out services in the 1980s – it is a new method, not a new end. The use of digital technology may bring about or represent changing politics and the form of technology-enabled decision-making may itself have certain consequences, but technology is no more than one tool in a state's toolbox (and it is certainly not a tool with magical properties which can somehow circumvent questions of politics).[55] The basic task of public lawyers remains, as Sir Ivor Jennings put it in 1936, to 'advise as to the technical devices which are necessary to make the policy efficient and to provide justice for individuals.'[56]

A starting point

Having set out a framework for analysing the progressive encroachment of technology in administrative justice, the following chapters offer my analysis of three significant, recent developments. My ambition is that the framework used here will be a robust way for others approaching the digitalisation of administrative justice to analyse what can often seem, especially for those working at the frontlines of these changes, tricky to assess at a macro level. On the basis of the analysis presented in the next three chapters, I suggest practical recommendations for each area.

My analysis in this book is a starting point in at least two senses – one practical and one more significant. At this early stage in the digitalisation of administrative justice, there is a limited evidence base to operate on, and further experiences with developing technologies may ultimately lead to different conclusions being drawn in the future. Moreover, any analysis of the digitalisation of administrative justice – the same as any position taken on the shape and function of the state – is open

---

[55] More will be said on this topic, in Chapter Four in particular.

[56] Jennings, William Ivor (1936) 'Courts and administrative law', *Harvard Law Review*, 49, 426, p 430.

to being contested.[57] For those who disagree with the arguments advanced here, my hope is that such disagreement provokes more detailed thinking on the important challenges presented by ensuring justice in an increasingly digital state.

---

[57] As Loughlin has pointed out, '[t]here is no metaphysical truth, there are no transcendent standards of correctness that lie outside the practices'; see Loughlin (2005), p 66 (note 11 above).

TWO

Crowdfunding and the changing dynamics of public interest judicial review

Judicial review is the system through which an individual ought to be able to go to a court and ask for a review of whether state action in respect of a certain issue is lawful. If the answer is no, there are various remedies the court can deploy to ensure government complies with the law. In performing this role, the courts are often said to be doing the job of upholding the Rule of Law. This simple account of judicial review is, as Harry Street once observed, 'a nice idea … but we just don't have it.'[1] This has been so for a range of reasons in recent history. Perhaps the primary failing of the present judicial review system is one of expense: judicial review is a 'Rolls-Royce' process that few can afford.[2] This state of affairs was recently described as 'public law's disgrace.'[3] It is while facing this reality that potential claimants

---

[1] Street, Harry (1975) *Justice in the Welfare State* (2nd edn), London: Stevens and Sons, p 65.

[2] Hickman, Tom (2017) 'Public law's disgrace', 9 February, UK Constitutional Law Blog, 9 February (https://ukconstitutionallaw.org/2017/02/09/tom-hickman-public-laws-disgrace).

[3] Ibid.

have started to use crowdfunding platforms to raise money in order to bring judicial review claims.[4] Crowdfunded claims have included high-profile 'public interest' challenges on new policies relating to junior doctors' pay[5] and the triggering of Brexit under Article 50 of the Treaty on European Union.[6] Although there is an increasing volume of crowdfunded judicial reviews, little has been said about this change – a shift which is, essentially, citizens using technology to gain access to an administrative justice processes in a way they may not have otherwise been able to.

In this chapter I explain how crowdfunding works and the changes in practice we have seen in recent years, particularly in relation to public interest judicial review cases. My argument is that these changes may be changing the model of public interest litigation from *closed* to *open*. I also argue that, while it may bring benefits of various kinds, in its present state crowdfunding is an unstable practice and, without some level of regulation, it risks unintended consequences.[7] I propose in this chapter that such

---

[4]   Hamman, Evan (2015) 'Save the reef! Civic crowdfunding and public interest environmental litigation', *Queensland University of Technology Law Review*, 15(1), 159; Gomez, Manuel, A. (2015) 'Crowdfunded justice: On the potential benefits and challenges of crowdfunding as a litigation financing tool', *University of San Francisco Law Review*, 49(2), 307; Elliot, Michael (2016) 'Trial by social-media: The rise of litigation crowdfunding', *University of Cincinnati Law Review*, 84(2), 529; Perry, Ronen (2018) 'Crowdfunding civil justice', *Boston College Law Review*, 59, 1357–95.

[5]   *Justice for Health v Secretary of State for Health* [2016] EWHC 2338; [2016] Med LR 599. See also Dyer, Clare (2016) 'Junior doctors' High Court challenge to Jeremy Hunt', *British Medical Journal*, 13 September, 354 (www.bmj.com/content/354/bmj.i4975).

[6]   See, for example, *R (Miller) v Secretary of State for Exiting the European Union* [2017] UKSC 5; [2017] 2 WLR 583; *R (Webster) v Secretary of State for Exiting the EU* [2018] EWHC 1543 (Admin).

[7]   I have developed wider aspects of this argument in more detail in Tomlinson, Joe (2019) 'Crowdfunding public interest judicial reviews: A risky new resource and the case for a practical ethics', *Public Law*, 166.

regulation ought to be orientated at lawyers who bring or act in crowdfunded judicial review cases.

The developing use of crowdfunding for judicial review

Within the context of a policy of fiscal austerity,[8] recent years have seen the government claim to have concerns about the expense of the justice system, and judicial review has been part of this. In a judicial review case, the government incurs two main costs, which are, of course, ultimately met by the taxpayer: first, defending the claim; and second, providing funds to support the court system in processing the case (for example, the provision of a hearing venue, a judge and court staff). At the same time of justice budgets being cut, there was talk of judicial review being a forum for 'weak or ill-founded claims' that were taking up 'large amounts of judicial time and costing the court system money.'[9] Subsequently, there were reforms that sought to restrict access to judicial review.[10] Reforms to the judicial review process were also completed in a context where funding cuts across the justice system were being made. For instance, there was a vast reduction in the amount of legal aid available to publicly fund cases. These changes had consequences for the bringing of judicial reviews.

Making sense of the economics of the judicial review process is no easy task. There is a complex landscape of costs rules, courts

---

[8] For an overview and analysis of the effects of austerity on the wider administrative justice system, see Thomas, Robert and Tomlinson, Joe (2017) 'Mapping current issues in administrative justice: austerity and the "more bureaucratic rationality" approach', *Journal of Social Welfare and Family Law*, 39(3), 380–99.

[9] Ministry of Justice (2012) 'Judicial review consultation', Press release, 13 December (www.gov.uk/government/news/judicial-review-consultation).

[10] Ministry of Justice (2014) *Judicial Review: Proposals for Further reform*, Cm 8703; Criminal Justice and Courts Act 2015.

fees, cost caps and other features, which are all interconnected.[11] There is only limited empirical evidence on how this economic dimension of judicial plays out in practice.[12] Crowdfunding is connected with this wider economic landscape in multiple ways, but it is primarily a funding method.

For those trying to fund a judicial review, there are a few options at present. You could simply pay privately if you have deep enough pockets. You will have to, typically, pay the costs of a solicitor and counsel on an hourly basis. Alternatively, you may be able to agree a fixed fee in advance. However, some lawyers may be unwilling to provide fixed fee arrangements if a case is unpredictable or they have not had the opportunity to fully develop a view on the nature and merits of the case. Because of this, sometimes fees are fixed initially, but if the claim is successful, then full fees as paid (something usually called a discounted fee agreement). A conditional fee agreement is also possible – sometimes referred to as 'no win now fee agreements'.[13] If a claim fails, a claimant may also need to cover the costs of the government's legal fees, or part of them.

How much a judicial review costs varies widely from case to case. If a case settles early, costs may be limited. But if it goes to a full hearing, they may be considerable. One estimate, from 2007, suggests that a typical judicial review can incur costs from

---

[11] Low Beer, Ravi and Tomlinson, Joe (2018) *Financial Barriers to Judicial Review*, London: Public Law Project.

[12] Bondy, Varda, Platt, Lucinda and Sunkin, Maurice (2015) *The Value and Effects of Judicial Review: The Nature of Claims, their Outcomes and Consequences*, London: Public Law Project.

[13] Lawyers are able to charge a success fee of up to 100% if the case is won to compensate them for the risk of being paid nothing. However, since April 2013, success fees are no longer recoverable from the defendant, but must instead be paid by the claimant. Given the non-monetary nature of judicial review, the prospect of paying a success fee often makes a conditional fee agreement expensive and unattractive.

£10,000 to £20,000.[14] However, complex cases can be much more expensive. In 2017, Tom Hickman, a judicial review practitioner, suggested that a 'very simple' case that took a two-hour hearing would cost around £8,000 to £10,000.[15] By contrast, a 'moderately complex claim lasting a day and not brought against a central government department' could cost beyond £40,000. For a 'substantial' judicial review heard over two days, Hickman estimates costs will run to between £80,000 and £200,000. There is no clear data on this, but it is clear that costs for cases that go to a full hearing can be significant.

Public funding, in the form of legal aid, is available for some cases.[16] The rules relating to legal aid are incredibly complex. Broadly speaking, to get funding a claimant has to be 'within scope' and eligible for legal aid,[17] satisfy a means test,[18] and prove that the merits of the claim are sufficient to satisfy the merits test.[19] In recent years, access to legal aid has been restricted and the overall budget vastly reduced. This has caused great concern

---

[14] Public Law Project (2007) *How to Fund a Judicial Review Claim When Public Funding Is Not Available*, London: Public Law Project, para 1, which was informed by a discussion with practitioners. Further and similar estimates are available in a response to a Ministry of Justice consultation made available via a Freedom of Information Act 2000 (FOIA) request; see FOIA Request No 171204020.

[15] Hickman (note 2 above).

[16] Legal aid grants also come with a level of costs protection. Before the event insurance policies (typically included in home and motor insurance policies) fund various types of litigation, but are ill suited to non-monetary claims where remedies are discretionary, and so are not generally available to cover judicial review proceedings.

[17] Legal Aid Sentencing and Punishment of Offenders Act 2012, Sections 9 and 10.

[18] Civil Legal Aid (Financial Resources and Payment for Services) Regulations 2013 (SI 2013/480) (as amended).

[19] Civil Legal Aid (Merits Criteria) Regulations 2013 (SI 2013/104) (as amended).

about an access to justice crisis.[20] In respect of judicial review in particular, Hickman has argued powerfully that they are part of an access to justice crisis that is 'public law's disgrace.'[21] He suggests that the ground-level reality is that 'people who have £169.15 or more per week for themselves and their family to live off, or who have any significant assets, do not qualify for legal aid.'[22] Available data indicates that there are now considerably fewer judicial reviews supported by legal aid than just a few years ago.[23]

Overall, the landscape for judicial review funding is, at present, one where resources have become scarce. However, costs are still high. Public interest judicial review (that is, those cases that seek to raise points of general public importance or change an approach to an issue) also finds itself within that landscape. There is now an extensive literature which discusses public interest litigation and the availability of funding – and the expense of courts processes more broadly – is widely discussed as a key factor in what litigation is actually brought.[24] As funding becomes scarcer, litigation that makes wider public interest arguments

---

[20] This was clear in the discussion around the Bach Commission; see The Bach Commission (2017) *The Right to Justice: The Final Report of the Bach Commission*, Fabian Policy Report, London: Fabien Society. See also Hickman (note 2 above).

[21] Hickman (note 2 above).

[22] Ibid.

[23] Data on this issue was made available under an FOIA request; see FOIA Request No 171020004.

[24] For an early example, see Vose, Clement (1959) *Caucasians Only*, Berkeley, CA: University of California Press, pp 119, 240. For a more recent discussion, see Hilson, Chris (2002) 'New social movements: The role of legal opportunity', *Journal of European Public Policy*, 9(2), 238–55; Andersen, Ellen Ann (2006) *Out of the Closets and Into the Courts: Legal Opportunity Structure and Gay Rights Litigation*, Ann Arbor, MI: University of Michigan Press; Vanhala, Lisa (2012) 'Legal opportunity structures and the paradox of legal mobilization by the environmental movement in the UK', *Law & Society Review*, 46(3), 523–56.

may also become more difficult.[25] It is in these conditions of greater scarcity and concerns about access to justice in which crowdfunding took off in the UK.

Crowdfunding is a method of raising money for a project via an online platform. The general use of crowdfunding across different parts of society has expanded rapidly in the last few years. It primarily emerged because, after the global financial crash of 2008, banks could not meet the demand for finance and an 'alternative finance economy' developed. This alternative finance economy is quickly becoming an important part of the UK economy.[26] In 2013, £666 million was raised in the UK through crowdfunding platforms. This went up to £1.74 billion and £3.2 billion in 2014 and 2015 respectively.[27] Government has also signalled its support for crowdfunding. In 2012, at a time of sweeping public spending cuts, the Coalition government invested £20 million in businesses via crowdfunding platforms and made a further £40 million investment in 2014.[28] Perhaps unsurprisingly, the speedy growth of this form of fundraising has left many questioning whether regulation now needs to adapt to these new activities.[29]

---

[25] Various third party funders – such as charitable trusts or the Equality and Human Rights Commission – still sometimes back judicial reviews, but the overall funding landscape remains more baron than it was in the recent past.

[26] Zhang, Brian, Baeck, Peter, Ziegler, Tanya, Bone, Jonathan and Garvey, Kieran (2015) *Pushing Boundaries: The 2015 UK Alternative Finance Industry Report*, Nesta.

[27] Ibid, p 11.

[28] BIS (Department for Business, Innovation & Skills) (2014) 'New £40 million investment by British Business Bank to support £450million of lending to smaller businesses', Press release, 25 February (www.gov.uk/government/news/new-40-million-investment-by-british-business-bank-to-support-450-million-of-lending-to-smaller-businesses).

[29] Armour, John and Enriques, Luca (2018) 'The promise and perils of crowdfunding: Between corporate finance and consumer contracts', *Modern Law Review*, 81(1), 51–84. The Financial Conduct Authority is also now

As a method of litigation funding, crowdfunding is best seen as a form of third party funding.[30] Historically this type of funding was prohibited, but the rules changed in recent decades, and now third party funding is seen as a key part of the justice system.[31] Lord Justice Jackson, in his landmark review of civil litigation costs, considered that third party funding is in principle 'beneficial and should be supported', because, among other benefits, it 'provides an additional means of funding litigation and, for some parties, the only means of funding litigation [and thus] promotes access to justice.'[32] With crowdfunding, money donated through the online platform forms a fund, which is the third party funder of the case. Some have drawn a distinction between 'investment-based' crowdfunding models, where investors have a financial stake in a monetary claim and seek to make profit, and 'non-investment-based' crowdfunding models, where the investor's reward is non-monetary or non-existent.[33]

There are multiple players on the UK crowdfunding scene at present. Two seem particularly important in the context of judicial review. First, there is CrowdJustice, an organisation

---

taking various steps in respect of crowdfunding platforms. For instance, it considers certain forms of crowdfunding – loan-based crowdfunding and investment-based crowdfunding – to be regulated activities under the Financial Services and Markets Act 2000.

[30] This was defined by Lord Justice Jackson as funding by a 'party who has no pre-existing interest in the litigation, usually on the basis that (i) the funder will be paid out of the proceeds of any amounts recovered as a consequence of the litigation, often as a percentage of the recovery sum; and (ii) the funder is not entitled to payment should the claim fail'; see Lord Justice Jackson (2009) *Review of Civil Costs: Final Report*, p xv.

[31] For an overview, see Lord Neuberger (2013) 'From Barretry, Maintenance and Champerty to Litigation Funding', Harbour Litigation Funding Lecture (www.supremecourt.uk/docs/speech-130508.pdf). See also Radin, Max (1935) 'Maintenance by Champerty', *California Law Review*, 24, 48–78, p 49; *Giles v Thompson* [1994] 1 AC 142, p 153 (Lord Mustill).

[32] Lord Justice Jackson, p 117 (note 30 above).

[33] Perry (note 4 above).

that provides and manages an online platform for those seeking to raise funds for a case. CrowdJustice allows 'case owners' to develop a page on the its website, to promote the case and facilitate online donations. On these pages, there is a target amount and deadline. These pages can then be circulated online to encourage donations. CrowdJustice does not offer legal advice – it simply facilitates the fundraising. The platform requires that users of the site have instructed a qualified lawyer and leaves the details of the case, and how it is presented to the public, to individual case owners. If a funding target is met, CrowdJustice takes a 6% 'platform fee', plus VAT, from the overall total raised, and transfers the rest into the case owner's solicitors' client account. Where a target is not met, the platform does not take a fee, pledges are cancelled and donations are not taken. When a case goes forward but there is money left over, the money goes back to CrowdJustice, but the case owner can decide to put that to another case on the site or to the Access to Justice Foundation. In the case of donations beyond £1,000, donors have the option of a pro rata refund.

Another key organisation on the UK crowdfunding scene is the Good Law Project. This is not a crowdfunding platform but it is a new organisation that is, in essence, a creature of crowdfunding success. The director of the Good Law Project, Jolyon Maugham QC, had a career as a successful tax barrister before he gained significant traction on social media. He used crowdfunding to fund judicial reviews he was bringing that had some wider political motivation. These activities evolved into the Good Law Project. It is an expressly political project, which seeks to drive social change through litigation.[34] Its focus areas include tax, workers' rights and Brexit. The first case the Good Law Project was involved centred on the argument regarding

---

[34] Details of the background of the organisation are set out in Maugham, Jolyon QC (2017) 'The Lawyer as Political Actor', Annual Queen Mary University of London Law and Society Lecture.

the Brexit process ultimately decided by the Supreme Court in *Miller*.[35] The argument in this case was famously published in a blog shortly after the referendum.[36] Maugham then crowdfunded initial advice on the basis of the blog (although this was one of multiple efforts around the same issue). After that initial foray, cases have included a high-profile challenge to the Electoral Commission's response to accusations of misconduct in the Brexit referendum.[37]

Beyond the high-profile work of Mr Maugham QC, the crowdfunding community more widely is ambiguous. Further research on who is involved and their experiences could shine fresh light on how this new platform is being used.

Emerging politics of crowdfunding

The emerging politics around crowdfunding is complicated. There are various strands that interact at various points. First, there is the politics of particular crowdfunded campaigns. The politics of campaigns are, quite naturally, often specific to the case. Challenges around Brexit have, in recent years, been a particular hotspot for successful campaigns. These campaigns have large groups of receptive and politically active donors. However, some campaigns pursued via crowdfunded cases can also bring up local issues. Given the need to campaign and given that crowdfunding requires donors that are capable of accessing and using the internet, social media has become a key space for

---

[35] *R (Miller) v Secretary of State for Exiting the European Union* (see note 6 above).

[36] The legal argument was outlined in Barber, Nick, Hickman, Tom and King, Jeff (2016) 'Pulling the Article 50 "trigger": Parliament's indispensable role', UK Constitutional Law Blog, 27 June (https://ukconstitutionallaw. org/2016/06/27/nick-barber-tom-hickman-and-jeff-king-pulling-the-article-50-trigger-parliaments-indispensable-role).

[37] *R (The Good Law Project) v Electoral Commission & Others* [2018] EWHC 2414 (Admin).

the expression of the political components of crowdfunding. Often, individuals leading crowdfunding campaigns seek to engage in public debate on platforms such as Twitter, both as part of wider campaigning activities but also to draw attention to the crowdfunded case. This raises the question of whether the campaigning is for the case or whether the case is an instrument of political campaigning. Traditional public interest litigation organisations have typically been more restrained in engaging in political argument in the social media and crowdfunding contexts. Instead, they typically adopt conventional campaigning practices with integrated crowdfunding links.

Beyond the politics of individual case campaigns, the crowdfunding platforms responsible for hosting and administering campaigns have particular objectives. For instance, CrowdJustice states its mission to be 'to give more access to the legal system. We're a team of lawyers, technologists and campaigners and we built CrowdJustice as a way to level the playing field.' The platform is an important player as it exerts control over the form of campaigns and how they are administered. So far, key platforms seem to be acting independently, professionally and in a manner consistent with traditional organisations concerned with issues such as access to justice. However, the 'mission' aspect of the platform is still an emerging dynamic, and it will be interesting to see how this area evolves in the coming years.

As for the government, there appears to be no clear policy position on crowdfunding justice. As noted above, government has promoted crowdfunding in other areas of policy but has not yet gone so far in the justice sphere. On the one hand, supporting crowdfunding may be an attractive policy for a government that has dramatically cut public funding for the justice system in recent years. If crowdfunding is a success, this may lead to a view that is could be a useful substitute for public funding in some circumstances.[38] On the other hand, supporting crowdfunding in the justice system may lead, especially with recent spending cuts in mind, to a view that crowdfunding is a second-rate substitute for legal aid. There is no evidence at all that crowdfunding is or could be an effective like-for-like substitute for public funding.

How crowdfunding integrates into the government's general policies on judicial review is also yet to be seen. In respect of the judicial review, the government wears two hats as principal designer and constant participant in the process. This means that it exerts a large degree of control over the judicial review process and can react to new developments. If there is a growth in public interest judicial review due to crowdfunding or crowdfunding has negative effects on how such judicial reviews are managed, there could be long-term effects. Harlow and Rawlings have mapped this terrain well. They explain that government can take action to restrict litigation through 'clamping down.'[39] This is a 'process' that involves 'structural or procedural change to the judicial review process or, put differently, procedural constraint designed to blunt substantive legal action.' If many crowdfunded cases are poorly managed, it is difficult to imagine a clamp down of some kind not happening.

---

[38] Some argue, however, that public funding may not be necessary in the way many often suggest; see Higgins, Andrew (2017) 'The costs of civil justice and who pays', *Oxford Journal of Legal Studies*, 37(3), 687–713. There is also a powerful argument for considering judicial review costs as distinct from standard civil disputes; see Fordham, Michael (2009) 'Rethinking costs in judicial review', *Judicial Review*, 306; *R (Davey) v Aylesbury Vale District Council* [2007] EWCA Civ 1166; [2008] 1 WLR 878 [18] (Sedley LJ).

[39] Harlow, Carol and Rawlings, Richard (2016) '"Striking Back" and "Clamping Down": An Alternative Perspective on Judicial Review', in John Bell, Mark Elliott, Jason N.E. Varuhas and Philip Murray (eds) *Public Law Adjudication in Common Law Systems: Process and Substance*, Oxford: Hart Publishing, Chapter 13.

The views on crowdfunding within the judiciary may also be significant in the long term. Much of judicial review remains discretionary. In practice, this means that judicial attitudes and thought can have meaningful impacts in cases. In terms of possible negative consequences, crowdfunding may risk irritating the judiciary by bringing explicitly political campaigning to the courts. There have also been concerns expressed about the effects of crowdfunding on litigation behaviour, such as it leading to grandstanding by lawyers. More broadly, increasing use of crowdfunding may generate unrealistic expectations that claimants should crowdfund if they require litigation funding. However, judges may also be receptive to crowdfunding as a means of increasing access to justice, and there are past examples of the judiciary liberalising gateways for public interest litigation.[40] Moreover, there are already examples of the judiciary reacting positively to crowdfunding.[41]

The politics of crowdfunding is incredibly diverse and complex. It is still also in a formative stage and we can expect further crystallisation of different views in the coming years, as the experience with crowdfunded judicial reviews grows. What is remarkable, even at this point, is that there are very few (public) critical voices on crowdfunding.

From a closed to open model of public interest judicial review

The growing use of crowdfunding forces us to revisit traditional models of judicial review.[42] In particular, it is perhaps changing how we ought to understand public interest judicial review.

---

[40] See, for example, *R (Corner House Research) v Secretary of State for Trade and Industry* [2005] EWCA Civ 192.

[41] See, for example, *Stephen Hawking and others v Secretary of State for Health & Social Care and National Health Service Commissioning Board* (unreported), 22 February 2018.

[42] There is limited modelling work on judicial review. The key authority on this is Rawlings, Richard (2008) 'Modelling judicial review', *Current Legal Problems*, 61(1), 95–123, p. 109.

In recent decades, public interest judicial reviews in the UK have often been brought by organisations with expertise of such litigation (for example, Liberty or JUSTICE) or some particular policy area (for example, Greenpeace). This litigation, being complex, expensive and unpredictable, was treated very carefully. Indeed, the same few organisations were frequent players. These organisations, it was often observed, had similar missions. Public interest litigation conducted by such organisations usually involved experienced lawyers and senior members of the organisation. Organisations, in the conduct of litigation, had various pressures that generally led them to litigate with discipline and care. For instance, they were often accountable to a board, and sometimes their wider membership. In a sense, we could say that this was a *closed* model of public interest judicial review. This is not meant in a pejorative sense, but is rather to say the activity was almost a niche and a specialist one. As a result, it was a relatively stable area of litigation overall.

With crowdfunding, the closed model of public interest litigation could be dislodged if there are more cases brought by litigants from outside of the traditional group of actors. It has always been the case that, if a person had sufficient funds, they could use their own funds to challenge government via judicial review.[43] Yet, the promise of crowdfunding is that it can overcome financial barriers to judicial review for the wider population. In so doing, it is likely that public interest judicial review in the UK – as an area of litigation – may become more diversified if crowdfunding continues to grow in importance. New focus areas for litigation may arise. New groups and people may become involved. In this way, crowdfunding may produce a shift from a closed to a more *open* model of public interest litigation in the UK. However, at the same time, the

---

[43] The spread-betting tycoon Stuart Wheeler, who challenged the UK's ratification of the Lisbon Treaty, is a good example; see *R (Wheeler) v Office of the Prime Minister* [2008] EWHC 1409 (Admin); [2008] ACD 70.

structures that made patterns of public interest litigation relatively stable in recent years may not be present in the same ways. The story is therefore more nuanced than simply the potential democratisation and diversification of public interest litigation.

Design considerations for an institutional response

The design of crowdfunding is a difficult topic as the state has done little to address this quickly developing sphere of legal activity. In the absence of a formal state institution of which to examine the design, here I provide a survey of some of the key considerations that may go to informing any future design.

It is clear crowdfunding can work in some cases. Some cases have raised vast amounts of money. However, success is far from guaranteed. For a crowdfunding campaign to be a success, there needs to be willing donors who are in a position to donate money. Sometimes, it may be the case that significant time and even money is required to bring attention to the campaign. This may not be so difficult if the issue already has a high profile but, for some, it could be a key barrier to crowdfunding. For those who are bringing claims that may not have a high level of popularity (such as claims by prisoners), crowdfunding may be of little utility. The central design question for any institutional response to crowdfunding is how to provide an effective framework to ensure risks are managed while benefits are optimised.

Crowdfunding campaign web pages are incredibly variable, and the extent of the variation demonstrates how the practicalities of managing a crowdfunded case give rise to some difficult ethical and strategic questions for lawyers. One key issue is when fundraising should take place. Asking for funding for a case can be speculative at an early stage of litigation, but there is only a short time window (typically three months) in which judicial reviews can be brought. There is also the issue of how much should be crowdfunded. A tension may arise here between the aims of not wanting to raise more than is necessary from the public and wanting to know that a case is properly funded. It has been argued that there may be a 'useful discipline' in 'putting yourself in a position where you have to make an ongoing case for people to support the litigation.'[44] The presentation of the crowdfunding pitch also raises some tricky questions. Crowdfunding campaigns are directed to the public, and therefore there is a need for them to be put in simple terms. However, some may suggest that, given this is a legal case seeking funding, details of the claims and evidence being put are required. Some crowdfunding attempts only give very broad overviews of the case they intend to bring, whereas others provide detailed pleadings and other documents. Related to this, some crowdfunding campaigns provide clear updates on the progress of a case, with new documents, whereas others do not. At the moment, practice in the management of crowdfunded cases seems to vary significantly. The need for a consistent baseline of ethical practice is an important question for any institutional framework in this area.

With the possible shift from a more closed to a more open model of public interest judicial review that crowdfunding may bring, there is the chance of new actors to come on to the scene. Jolyon Maugham QC is a good example of the possibility of crowdfunding opening up who is involved in public interest litigation.[45] As noted above, organisations that have traditionally been active in public interest judicial reviews had various pressures which generally led them to litigate with discipline and care (for example, being accountable to a board and their membership). These structures are not necessarily replicated for Mr Maugham QC and others following in his footsteps. Crowdfunders are more likely to see themselves as accountable to their base of donors: 'if you are asking people to dip their hands

---

44 Maugham (note 34 above).
45 Ibid.

into their pockets to fund a case you need to be able to justify that decision to yourself – and to them.'[46] With this change, there may be changes to the practice of public interest judicial review in some cases. Any institutional response to crowdfunding must consider the dynamics of this new landscape.

An important distinction can also be drawn between 'investment-based' crowdfunding models, where investors have a financial stake in a monetary claim, and 'non-investment based' crowdfunding models, where the investors' reward is non-monetary or intangible.[47] Ronan Perry argues that investment-based crowdfunding is more secure as the incentives of the person putting their money into the case provides a kind of filtering, whereas in judicial review cases, where claims are primarily about the legality of government action and not monetary compensation, there is less of an incentive for donors to properly examine the merits of a case.[48] Perry recommends that in non-investment-based crowdfunding models, claims should be subject to a professional vetting process to minimise the risk of generating unmeritorious claims. Different organisations involved with crowdfunding take different approaches to vetting. As outlined above, CrowdJustice requires that every individual or group taking a case either has a qualified solicitor or barrister who has been instructed, or that the case is being taken by a non-profit organisation. The Good Law Project uses the resources of its director for this purpose. What level of vetting is required and how to ensure it in practice are key design questions.

Recommendations

Overall, crowdfunding represents a risky resource. It has the potential to generate unforeseen consequences by disrupting

---

46 Ibid.

47 Perry (note 4 above).

48 Ibid.

relatively stable patterns and practices of public interest judicial review litigation. Equally, however, crowdfunding has helped support valuable cases that would not otherwise have been brought. The cost of judicial review, and the diminished public funding available for it, make crowdfunding potentially more important. Given the contrasting aspects of crowdfunding, the challenge for any institutional response is to design frameworks that promote optimisation while minimising risk. I have argued elsewhere that regulation ought to be focused on lawyers as they possess the most significant amount of power in the bringing and conduct of crowdfunded judicial reviews.[49] I have also suggested that guidance on the form of regulation can be derived from looking at existing professional codes.[50] There is no need to place a straitjacket on litigation strategy, but setting a general ethical baseline similar to those seen in existing professional codes would be beneficial.

Going forward, ethical regulation of crowdfunding, based on detailed consultation with relevant stakeholders, should be considered by the appropriate regulators. For this exercise to be as effective as possible, a more robust empirical evidence base would be hugely beneficial. In the interim, key organisations involved in public interest judicial reviews should consider developing their own policies on responsible practices for crowdfunding for litigation.

---

[49] Tomlinson (note 7 above).

[50] See Bar Standards Board (2018) *Handbook* (3rd edn), p 22; SRA (Solicitors Regulation Authority) (2017) *SRA Handbook* (Version 19). For an example of a recent technology-led amendment, see Bar Standards Board (2017) 'Guidance for barristers using social media', February (www.barstandardsboard.org.uk/media/1821624/bsb_social_media_guidance_pdf.pdf).

THREE

The tribunals gamble

As the role of technology steadily grows in justice systems around the world,[1] the UK Ministry of Justice (MoJ) and HMCTS have taken the step of being global pioneers.[2] They are now in the process of putting many court and tribunal processes – as well as court administration systems – on to a digital footing. Tribunals – which hear many more challenges to the decisions of public authorities than the courts do via judicial review – are a major focus of these changes.[3] Reforms to tribunals are expected to involve tribunal appeals being lodged, and potentially determined, online, with the idea of parties coming into contact with each other and a judge at an earlier stage than before. The spur for these changes is a government drive to cut the running

---

[1] See, for example, Katsh, Ethan and Rabinovich-Einy, Orna (2017) *Digital Justice*, Oxford: Oxford University Press; Barton, Benjamin H. and Bibas, Stephanos (2017) *Rebooting Justice*, New York: Encounter Books.

[2] For an overview of the entire reform project, see Rozenberg, Joshua (2018) *The Online Court: Will IT Work?*, Guildford: Legal Education Foundation.

[3] Ministry of Justice (2016) *Transforming Our Justice System*, London, p 15. My focus here excludes party-to-party tribunals, such as the Employment Tribunal – the focus is solely on claims concerning administrative decisions.

costs of the justice system.[4] As such, new online procedures are being coupled with court closures and significant reductions in the amount of court staff.[5] While there is hope that online processes may increase access to justice for many, there is also concern that some may be digitally excluded from justice. At the same time, there is a worry that new online processes will not compensate adequately for reduced service provision in respect of traditional processes. Overall, these reforms represent a major policy gamble by a government under pressure to reduce costs: the gamble that technology-based solutions can provide more access to justice for significantly less money.

Tribunal reform is starting in the Social Security and Child Support Tribunal (SSCS) and then moving on to the First-tier Tribunal (Immigration and Asylum) Chamber (FtTIAC).[6] This chapter starts by looking at the role of tribunals in those two contexts. In particular, it is highlighted how the role of tribunals within the wider administrative justice landscape has been significantly reduced in recent years. I then explain different stances – from the enthusiastic to the cynical – on the reforms, before explaining how online processes are likely to change the face of the traditional model of tribunals that many are familiar with at present. The final part of the chapter considers some of the key design issues arising as part of these reforms, before offering some recommendations on the ongoing reform process.

Development of online tribunals

As outlined in Chapter Two, there has been a significant reduction in the amount of public money that the government

---

4 Ryder, Ernest (2018) 'Assisting Access to Justice', University of Keele.

5 National Audit Office (2018) *Early Progress in Transforming Courts and Tribunals*, HC 1001, Session 2017–2019; House of Commons Committee of Public Accounts (2018) *Transforming Courts and Tribunals*, HC 976.

6 HM Courts & Tribunals Service (2018) *Reform Update: Autumn 2018.*

is willing to spend on the justice system since 2010. There is now a wide concern that the justice system is under-funded, and this has carried the consequence of substantially reduced access to justice for many people, particularly those without means and those who are vulnerable.[7] The court and tribunal reform programme has been developed in response to these budget cuts and austerity more broadly. This modernisation programme – which covers a wide variety of reforms – aims to redesign and modernise the way in which people can access courts and tribunals by introducing online and digital processes. It also seeks to create efficiencies by moving a paper-heavy system of administration on to a new digital basis. The pressure from the Treasury to reduce spending looms large over the reforms.

The reform programme was announced in September 2016 in a joint vision statement entitled *Transforming Our Justice System*, published in the joint names of the Lord Chancellor, the Lord Chief Justice and the Senior President of Tribunals.[8] This paper highlights the need for radical reform required to modernise and upgrade the justice system through technology. It states that there is a compelling case for reform of tribunals:

> Tribunals will be digital by default, with easy to use and intuitive online processes put in place to help people lodge a claim more easily, but with the right levels of help in place for anyone who needs it, making sure that nobody is denied justice.[9]

The idea is that tribunal users will be placed at the heart of the system, and tribunal judges and members will move towards a more inquisitorial and problem-solving approach.

---

[7] See, for example, JUSTICE (2015) *Delivering Justice in an Age of Austerity.*

[8] Lord Chancellor, the Lord Chief Justice and the Senior President of Tribunals (2016) *Transforming Our Justice System*, Ministry of Justice.

[9] Ibid, p 15.

Documents relevant to appeals can be shared via E-platforms, cutting administration costs and delay – allowing appeals to be determined or otherwise resolved quicker than is possible in any paper-based system. It is also said that there will be the adoption of 'continuous online hearings', where judges are involved much sooner in appeals, are enabled to oversee evidence assimilation and are put in a position to make decisions at an earlier stage in an appeal process where possible. This was the broad vision that served as the starting point: it was light on detail but heavy on ambition.

There are a wide variety of tribunals and they operate in very different contexts – applying different law, dealing with different government bodies, possessing particular cultures of adjudication etc. The *Transforming Our Justice System* paper told us that online appeals processes would be trialled in SSCS. This being the largest tribunal jurisdiction and one where appellants have a wide variety of complex needs, there was a 'if we can do it there, we can do it anywhere' spirit adopted. FtTIAC would be next in the queue. Beyond this, however, little was known about how the reforms would be implemented and what online appeals processes would look like. Even at the time of writing, the full details are yet to emerge (2019). It is still important to understand the context in which tribunals have operated to grasp the potential implications of digitalisation, whatever form it takes. Here, I focus on the recent context of two of the largest tribunals, which are also the first two to be put online: SSCS and FtTIAC.

Social security policy is administered by officials within the Department for Work and Pensions (DWP), who take approximately 12 million decisions each year to determine whether or not claimants are eligible for benefits. The two benefits with the largest number of claimants are Employment and Support Allowance (ESA) and Personal Independence Payments (PIPs). After a claim is made, an assessment will be undertaken, usually involving a 'healthcare professional' who is employed by a private provider under contract with the DWP.[10] Some decisions are refused and some of those refusals are disputed by claimants through mandatory reconsideration (MR) (around 300,000 per year) and tribunal appeals (around 150,000 per year).

There are often concerns with the quality of both the decision process as well as the adverse outcomes for the individuals concerned. In relation to initial decision-making processes and assessments, the contracting out of assessments to private companies, such as ATOS and Maximus, has been widely criticised.[11] Criticism of initial decision-making has also emerged from the senior judiciary. Sir Ernest Ryder, Senior President of Tribunals, has stated that most appeals are based on bad decisions.[12] He found that the quality of evidence offered by the DWP at tribunals would often be 'wholly inadmissible' in any other court, and that 60% of cases were 'no-brainers' where there was nothing in the law or facts that would make the DWP win. This, the Senior President argued, meant poor decision-making led to 'an inappropriate use of judicial resources, it's an inappropriate experience for the users, and the cost is simply not right.' The DWP has defended its decision-making, and regularly attributes decisions overturned at appeal to new evidence – which was not before them – being presented at the tribunal. There have also been legal challenges to benefits decision-making. In 2017, the Administrative Court quashed a regulation relating to PIP decision-making on the basis that

---

[10] For a general discussion, see Thomas, Robert and Tomlinson, Joe (2017) 'Mapping current issues in administrative justice: Austerity and the "more bureaucratic rationality" approach', *Journal of Social Welfare and Family Law*, 39(3), 380–99, pp 396–7.

[11] House of Commons Work and Pensions Committee (2018) *PIP and ESA Assessments*, HC 829 2017-19.

[12] Dugan, Emily (2017) 'A senior judge has suggested charging the government for every "no-brainer" benefits case it loses in court', *BuzzFeed News*, 9 November.

it was discriminatory.[13] In response, the DWP decided not to appeal the judgment and to review the case of every person receiving PIP – a total of some 1.6 million individuals.

In 2013, the DWP also introduced MR to resolve disputes before they reach tribunals.[14] The justification was to resolve disputes quickly and to reduce the volume of tribunal appeals.[15] Claimants can no longer appeal directly to a tribunal, but must first request a MR.[16] Between 2013 and 2017, some 1.5 million MRs were decided. It transpired that MR was, in practice, very quick: average monthly clearance times did not go above 20 days.[17] However, MR has been criticised on various grounds. It has been suggested that it discourages many people from pursuing their claims before tribunals. There has been a steep drop in the volume of appeals lodged since the introduction of MR. In 2014/15, appeal numbers were 73% lower compared with 2013/14.[18] MR was intended as a filter, but the concern has been that many cases that could succeed before tribunals fall

---

[13] *R. (on the application of RF) v Secretary of State for Work and Pensions* [2017] EWHC 3375 (Admin). The regulation in question was the Social Security (Personal Independence Payment) (Amendment) Regulations 2017, Reg 2(4).

[14] It has been estimated that this review could cost £3.7 billion by 2023; see BBC News (2018) 'Personal independence payments: All 1.6 million claims to be reviewed', 30 January.

[15] DWP (Department for Work and Pensions) (2012) *Mandatory Consideration of Revision Before Appeal*, London.

[16] Welfare Reform Act 2012, Section 102; The Universal Credit, Personal Independence Payment, Jobseeker's Allowance and Employment and Support Allowance (Decisions and Appeals) Regulations SI 2013/381. A concurrent change was that whereas previously claimants lodged their appeals with the DWP, appeals are now lodged directly with the tribunal.

[17] DWP (Department for Work and Pensions) (2017) *Employment and Support Allowance: Work Capability Assessments, Mandatory reconsiderations and appeals*, London, September, p 7.

[18] The subsequent increase is largely accounted for by appeals lodged by claimants being transferred from Disability Living Allowance to Personal Independence Payments.

away after the MR stage. This creates the impression that the DWP is gatekeeping the tribunals system and taking advantage of claimant fatigue.[19] Particular concerns have often arisen due to the effect of MR on the behaviour of vulnerable claimants. Among the specific worries are that MR decision notices often simply restate the same reasons as were given for the initial decision without further detail, that the decision–making process is merely a 'rubber stamp' exercise, that tribunals often reach very different conclusions to the MR process, and that officials conducting MRs prefer the evidence of a contracted–in assessor to other legitimate medical evidence.[20] Such concerns are underscored by the fact that MR has the lowest satisfaction rating of any part of the DWP process, and that there have been much lower success rates for claimants in MR compared with tribunal appeals.[21] From 2013 to 2016 there were some one million MR decisions, with 17% being decided in favour of the claimant. Appeals success rates have, by comparison, been around 40%, rising to 65% in recent years.

It is within this changing context of social security adjudication that online tribunals are being introduced by HMCTS. The task of creating an effective online process for social security tribunals also engages a challenging demographic context. Many appellants are vulnerable and have physical and mental health

---

[19] A previous empirical study found that local authority officers could use administrative review to control claimants' access to tribunals; see Eardley, Tony and Sainsbury, Roy (1993) 'Managing appeals: The control of Housing Benefit internal reviews by local authority officers', *Journal of Social Policy*, 22(4), 461–85. Other evidence suggests that claimant fatigue often discourages people from challenging decisions; see Cowan, David and Halliday, Simon (2003) *The Appeal of Internal Review: Law, Administrative Justice, and the (Non-)Emergence of Disputes*, Oxford: Hart Publishing, pp 138–40.

[20] Social Security Advisory Committee (2016) *Decision Making and Mandatory Reconsideration*.

[21] DWP (Department for Work and Pensions) (2016) *DWP Claimant Service and Experience Survey 2014/15*, p 85.

issues. Furthermore, although the fiscal value of disputes in the tribunal may seem small, for many claimants the implications of appeals affect their living arrangements significantly.

Similar trends are visible in recent developments in the FtTIAC, including concerns about the quality of initial decision-making in the Home Office. In terms of the number of appeals that the FtTIAC receives, it has the second highest number of receipts of any First-tier Tribunal (SSCS being the largest tribunal jurisdiction). However, there has been a dramatic drop in the total number of appeals being lodged in the tribunal in recent years. In the first quarter of 2009/10, the FtTIAC received a total of 43,750 receipts. This decreased to just 11,864 receipts in the first quarter of the year 2018/19, representing a decrease of almost 73% in the total number of receipts of appeals received by the tribunal over that period.

Several factors may be in play in relation to the rapid decrease in the volume of appeals, and the trend is best explained by reference to a combination of them. However, the most obvious and main explanation is the systematic removal of appeal rights in certain categories of immigration decisions.[22] In 2014, immigration appeal rights (except those relating to asylum and human rights grounds) were replaced with a system of administrative review. The significant reduction in the tribunal's workload is the policy working as intended. The key motivation of the policy is that high success rates in tribunal appeals and their inconvenience to efficient administration both incurred costs and frustrated political ends.

The substitution of appeals to the tribunal for administrative review can cynically be viewed as limiting access to effective

---

[22] Immigration Act 2014, Section 15; Immigration Rules, Appendix AR. Family visitor appeals were abolished in 2013: Crime and Courts Act 2013, Section 52.

administrative redress as a mechanism for immigration control.[23] A more sympathetic interpretation would perhaps contend that administrative review is quicker and easier for immigration applicants compared to a tribunal appeal, and that as a process internal to administration, administrative review provides a better opportunity for the Home Office to systematically improve the quality of all decisions. While it is true that users may want quick and easy decisions,[24] and it is also true that administrative review is quick (typically a matter of a weeks), it would be naïve to see the preference for, and expansion of, administrative review within the context of immigration redress as simply a policy that promotes the interests of the applicants or efficient administration. There is a strong and well-founded concern that administrative reviews 'are neither independent nor transparent, but merely involve a different caseworker taking another look at the papers.'[25] Furthermore, within the context of immigration and asylum, the use of internal review processes has routinely been criticised as 'superficial' and 'ineffective' by oversight bodies, including by a parliamentary committee.[26]

As regards the new system of administrative review, the Independent Chief Inspector of Borders and Immigration concluded, in his first report on the system, that low-level, untrained and temporary staff with limited or no experience of

---

[23] Thomas, Robert (2016) 'Immigration and Access to Justice', in Ellie Palmer, Tom Cornford, Audrey Guinchard and Yseult Marique (eds) *Access to Justice: Beyond the Policies and Politics of Austerity*, Oxford: Hart Publishing, p 127, which speculates on the possibility of 'the end of appeals' in immigration redress.

[24] Berthoud, Richard and Bryson, Alex (1997) 'Social security appeals: What do the claimants want?', *Journal of Social Security Law*, 4, 17–41; Richardson, Genevra and Genn, Hazel (2007) 'Tribunals in transition', *Public Law*, 116.

[25] Thomas, p 126 (note 23 above).

[26] See, for example, House of Commons Constitutional Affairs Committee (2004) *Asylum and Immigration Appeals: Second Report of Session 2003–04*, HC 211-I.

immigration law were undertaking reviews.[27] At the same time, there was little oversight of these officials. Some less good review decisions demonstrated 'an over-reliance on the initial refusal decision letter.'[28] The reasoning of decisions was often brief and underdeveloped.[29] And unlike appeals before the FtTIAC, new evidence cannot be taken into account in a review.[30] This unresponsiveness is unsatisfactory in a context like immigration and asylum where there is a high possibility of the circumstances of an applicant changing between the initial adverse decision and the subsequent appeal or review.

As for the tribunal itself, recent years have been characterised by delays and high success rates. The length of time it takes to get an appeal decided is an important element of access to justice. One of the possible strengths of tribunals, relative to ordinary courts, is their potential to dispose of cases quickly. Across the tribunal, between the first and third quarter of 2017/18, the average age of an appeal at the time at which it is disposed exceeded, and stayed above, the 50-week threshold for those three quarters. The clear trend in the tribunal in recent years is towards longer waiting times. There are various possible explanations for why this is the case. It could be that there are more complex cases coming before the tribunal, but there appears to be no reason to think that appeals have become significantly more complex. Litigation behaviour could be changing. A possible decrease in representation may also be a factor. Equally, workload changes in the tribunals can be hard to predict, and ensuring there are sufficient judicial resource to

---

[27] ICIBI (Independent Chief Inspector of Borders and Immigration) (2016) *An Inspection of the Administrative Review Processes Introduced Following the Immigration Act 2014*. See also ICIBI (2017) *A Re-inspection of the Administrative Review Process*.

[28] Ibid, para 2.10.

[29] *R (Akturk) v Secretary of State for the Home Department* [2017] 4 WLR 62, [47] (Holamn J).

[30] Immigration Rules, Appendix AR [2.4].

meet demand can be difficult. Whatever the explanation, it is remarkable that during a period in which the number of appeals has dropped, the amount of time taken to decide appeals has increased substantially.

Success rates in the tribunal remain high and appear to be increasing further – close to 50% across the jurisdiction. The present success rates in the FtTIAC essentially create a situation where getting a tribunal hearing means that the chances of a favourable decision are almost 50/50. It is difficult to infer too much from basic outcomes data, but it likely shows that errors in Home Office decision-making are not uncommon. However, success rates could be explained by reference to tribunals having more evidence than initial decision-makers, or other differences in the two decision-making processes. Any blanket claim that all successful appeals reveal an avoidable mistake by the Home Office would therefore be incorrect. What is perhaps more noteworthy is the vast difference in success rates between administrative review and tribunal appeals. Under the old system, around 49% of appeals were successful, whereas in 2015/16, the success rate for administrative reviews conducted in the UK was 8%, falling to just 3.4% the year after.[31]

In a further reform with implications for the tribunal, there has been the introduction of the so-called 'deport first, appeal later' policy in human rights and asylum appeals. Provisions in the Immigration Act 2014 gave the Home Office the power to deport foreign nationals with criminal convictions without allowing them to appeal the deportation in the UK.[32] The Immigration Act 2016 then widened these powers to affect all

---

[31] For detailed analysis of recent evidence and data, see Thomas, Robert and Tomlinson, Joe (2019: forthcoming) 'A different tale of judicial power: Administrative review as a problematic response to the judicialisation of tribunals', *Public Law*.

[32] Nationality, Immigration and Asylum Act 2002, Section 94B, an amendment introduced by the Immigration Act 2014, Section 17(3).

migrants wishing to appeal on human rights grounds.[33] If an out-of-country appeal succeeds, the appellant may be able to return to the UK. Out-of-country appeals allow for speedier deportations and reduce the amount of detained immigration applicants. This reduces costs for the state. At the same time, the geographic separation of the applicant from the tribunal has a number of important consequences. Applicants are less likely to appeal. Establishing access to a tribunal may prove difficult from certain locations, including because of the expense of realising the right to appeal. It could also be more difficult to find and secure representation. For video-linked out-of-country appeal hearings, the hearing will be qualitatively different from a traditional oral hearing. Furthermore, it is highly likely that the applicant would have already experienced material harm from the administrative error as a consequence of the act of deportation. For example, the applicant may experience loss of employment or suffer detriment through remoteness from relations in the UK. Since the expansion of this policy, the Supreme Court has held that the out-of-country appeals process can be effectively fair for human rights purposes in the context of general criminal deportations.[34] However, if an appeal from abroad is not effective, then the public interest in removal would be outweighed and an application should not be certified.[35]

Overall, the move to online tribunals has to be understood as part of a series of important changes in recent years. Reforms have, broadly, led to tribunals having a diminished role within the wider system of administrative justice. This provides the context in which a politics around online tribunals has emerged.

---

[33] Immigration Act 2016, Section 63.

[34] *R (on the application of Kiarie) v Secretary of State for the Home Department* [2017] 1 WLR 2380.

[35] In a recent case, the Upper Tribunal gave guidance on the questions to be addressed in this respect; see *AJ (s 94B: Kiarie and Byndloss questions) Nigeria* [2018] UKUT 115 (IAC); [2018] Imm AR 976.

Politics of online tribunals

The politics of online tribunals largely spans a spectrum from cynics to enthusiasts. The core question in the digitalisation of tribunals is whether the reforms will, in time, improve both access to and the quality of administrative justice, or leave citizens in a worse-off position. Many hold strong views on the use of technology in the justice system, but great caution is required here: there is very little evidence on the impact of digital procedures in public justice systems, and many views are therefore heavily grounded in speculation. To think about the emerging politics around these reforms, it is helpful to imagine two broad views on the prospects of digitalisation: one where traditional tribunal justice is enhanced and another where digitalisation is just another step toward a weakened tribunal system. There are, of course, many increments between these two positions, but most commentators tend to lean towards one or the other viewpoint.

For the digitalisation enthusiasts, the prospect of online appeals presents the opportunity to resolve easy cases quickly and, in doing so, to reduce stress caused to appellants who are currently forced to endure long waiting times ahead of hearings. Digitalisation could also reduce the cost of administering tribunal appeals and reduce backlogs that build up over time. Evidence may be easy to submit and assimilate for both appellants and government bodies, while being easier to manage for judges. Communication about evidence between all parties could also be quicker, cheaper and more convenient. Appellants could save money by not travelling and taking time out of work, while government can save administration costs. Technology could also permit judicial resources to be flexibly deployed – allowing judges to work as efficiently as possible, in a way that most adds value to an appeal. It may even transpire that online appeals are cheaper than internal review systems and may make use of the tribunals appeals system more attractive to government departments. In redesigning tribunal processes for digitalisation, there is also the opportunity to do away with needless complexity and to provide accessible online processes. Online processes may be less intimidating for appellants. With the use of assisted digital services, there could be the creation of a wider support environment around tribunals that may not be present in the current process.[36]

At the other end of the optimism spectrum, a cynic may view the digitalisation of tribunals as having numerous significant pitfalls that could weaken administrative justice. At a basic level, it may be thought that hearings will not be as effective when managed online. They could, for instance, not be developed in a way that makes them useful for making (often complex) decisions of law and fact.[37] This could lead to more mistakes that have serious effects on the lives of citizens. There is also the risk that online appeals will lead to lower success rates than traditional appeals. Success rates between paper and oral appeals differ significantly, and online appeals could have similar consequences.[38] Use of video links and other remote communication methods may see appellants not participate

---

[36] Ministry of Justice (2017) *Transforming Our Justice System: Assisted Digital Strategy, Automatic Online Conviction and Statutory Standard Penalty, and Panel Composition in Tribunals: Government Response.* The government has contracted this job out to the Good Things Foundation. For the context on assisted digital, see JUSTICE (2018) *Preventing Digital Exclusion from Online Justice.*

[37] See the comments, for instance, in *R (Mohibullah) v Secretary of State for the Home Department* [2016] UKUT 561 (IAC) at [90]; *R (Kiarie and Byndloss)* (n 63) at [67]; and *Secretary of State for the Home Department v Nare* (evidence by electronic means) Zimbabwe [2011] UKUT 00443 (IAC) [17].

[38] For a discussion, see Thomas, Cheryl and Genn, Hazel (2013) *Understanding Tribunal Decision-making: A Foundational Empirical Study*, London: Nuffield Foundation.

as effectively in their cases.[39] At the same time, despite the possibility of savings through digitalisation, costs may ultimately rise overall. For appellants, they may, for instance, have to visit assisted digital centres multiple times. For those using a traditional oral hearing, journey times and costs may be increased by hearing centre closures. For government, if many appellants do not make use of the new online process, they may not see significant cost savings. Instead, there may just be another appeal mode with additional running costs incurred. Online appeals, hosted on the gov.uk website, may also risk losing the appearance of independence from the government departments that are the subject of appeals. In relation to assisted digital services, the uptake could be low or they could provide another gap in the tribunal appeal process where meritorious appeals fall out of the system. There is also the possibility that 'digital assistance' strays into giving inappropriate and unregulated legal advice.[40]

A new model of tribunal justice

The full details of online appeal procedures across different tribunal jurisdictions are yet to be seen. Moreover, the impacts of digitalisation will not be known without rigorous and extensive empirical research. However, on the basis of what is known so far, it is clear that digitalisation will see the creation of a *new online model* of tribunal which will, at first at least, sit alongside the present *traditional model*.[41]

---

[39] Federman, Mark (2006) 'On the media effects of immigration and Refugee Board hearings via videoconference', *Journal of Refugee Studies*, 19(4), 433; Eagly, Ingrid V. (2015) 'Remote adjudication in immigration', *Northwestern University Law Review*, 109(4), 933–1019.

[40] See the concerns set out in JUSTICE (2018) *Immigration and Asylum Appeals – A Fresh Look*, London: JUSTICE.

[41] For a fuller analysis of the changing models of tribunals in the UK, see Thomas, Robert (2017) 'Current Developments in UK Tribunals: Challenges for Administrative Justice', in Sarah Nason (ed) *Administrative Justice in*

The *traditional model* of tribunals has certain features that can be contrasted with the likely post-digitalisation model. The first obvious feature to note is that, at present, tribunals and their administration are paper-heavy. Some appeals are determined via an oral hearing, where appellants can put their case and judges can ask questions, and some are determined by a judge reviewing papers and evidence. Parties correspond over evidence – which, including between HMCTS and government bodies, is shared manually. A second key feature is that the process is designed around the hearing or determination. Evidence is gathered in time for the determination and the determination is then made in a form of a – typically very short – binding decision. Although there are important differences of detail, this is the broad traditional model of tribunal operating in SSCS and FtTIAC.

The traditional model of tribunals is now firmly established within the legal system. It has been broadly successful in dealing with a large caseload in a just and proportionate manner. It does, however, have multiple limitations. As the traditional model is designed around the formal determination, anticipation for the hearing can create stress for appellants over long periods of time. For cases with clear problems in the decision being appealed, this seems unnecessary. All of this can make tribunal appeals inefficient and inconvenient. There is typically little or no communication between the parties before the hearing. The hearing will usually be the first and only opportunity for the parties to exchange views and engage with the tribunal. Given the volume of cases and the need to list oral hearings, appeals can take some time to be heard and decided. For instance, in 2017, social security appeals took on average 20 weeks to be

Wales and Comparative Perspectives, Cardiff: University of Wales Press, Chapter 7.

decided whereas immigration appeals took 51 weeks.[42] Many weeks of 'downtime' pass in which nothing is happening to an appeal other than delay. A major issue for many appellants is not knowing how their appeal is progressing through the tribunal process. Weeks can go by without any sort of update. The consequent risk is that claimants disengage, miss deadlines or do not turn up to their hearings. This can lead to adjournments and further delays, which can further increase stress and anxiety for appellants.[43]Another drawback is that the demand on HMCTS to manage an enormous number of paper files by itself generates complications, such as lost and mislaid documents, thereby prompting complaints.[44]

The new online model moves away from the traditional model in a range of important ways – offering features that may offset some of the main limitations of the traditional model. Instead of paper-based appeals, appeals will originate online. The internal tribunal processes will also be based on automatically shared paperwork. These new processes will likely extend to the government departments that are the subject of the appeal, making information-sharing and hearing preparation quickly. As part of the move to a digital system, users will get updates via SMS and email on the progress of their appeal. All online processes and updates will use non-legal language. Perhaps the most significant change in the model will be the move to continuous online dispute resolution. As outlined above, this aims to bring all of the parties to an appeal as early as possible,[45]

---

[42] Ministry of Justice (2017) *Tribunals and Gender Recognition Statistics Quarterly, April to June 2017*, Table T3.

[43] Marchant, Robin (2017) 'Sometimes it makes sense to start in the middle', *Inside HMCTS*, 3 February.

[44] Parliamentary and Health Service Ombudsman (2016) *Complaints about UK Government Departments and Agencies, and Some UK Public Organisations 2015–16*, p 17.

[45] This model has been pioneered by the Traffic Penalty Tribunal and is to be piloted in social security appeals. The Traffic Penalty Tribunal also uses telephone hearings and, to a lesser degree, traditional physical hearings.

allowing the key issues to be identified quickly and for 'easy' cases to be determined without the need to wait for a traditional hearing. This removes the 'hearing-centric' component of the traditional tribunal model, replacing it with a more conversation mode of decision-making that allows the parties to informally consider issues.

How the new online model of tribunals will work in practice is presently unclear and it will likely vary across different tribunal jurisdictions. What is clear is that operationalising this new model of tribunals presents multiple important questions of design. The next part of this chapter turns to map some of the key design issues.

Key design issues

As online tribunal processes are still in development, it is not yet possible to map the issues that have arisen with their design. It is possible, however, to highlight some of the key issues arising in the ongoing design process. I cover eight of the most important issues here.

First, there is the question of which appeals should be channelled through online processes and which should not. Are there some types of cases that would not be appropriate for online dispute resolution? If so, which types of cases? How precisely would those cases be identified? Through a blanket policy or on a case-by-case basis? What approach will be taken when cases raise issues of the appellant's credibility? It is clear, and the government understands, that many cases will simply not be suitable for online procedures. It is also suggested by the government that appellant consent to use of online processes will be a key principle, and that appellants will not be forced into online processes. How and when such channelling decisions are made will be an essential design question.

Second, there is the key design issue of how traditional values of legal process and good administration – such as transparency, fairness, participation, judicial independence and open justice – are transferred to the digital sphere.[46] How will these values be effectively respected in the digital sphere? For instance, how will the value of open justice be secured through an online process? These values – loaded with varied concerns and preferences about what a good justice system looks like – will animate views on online appeals, and process designs must consider them and develop appropriate responses. This may raise some difficult trade-offs between different value preferences, but also straightforwardly tricky questions of how to operationalise certain values in the digital context. For instance, the implementation of effective open justice in an online tribunal process will require practical design innovation.[47]

Third, there is the design of communication platforms. It is expected that online messaging systems will be used. Experience in the Traffic Penalty Tribunal – an early pioneer of online appeals – has found that online messaging has considerable advantages in terms of quickly narrowing down the issues and enabling a focused exchange of views. Online messaging can significantly lower the costs, delays and constraints that come with physical hearings. Having all the information and evidence together in a single online file as opposed to a paper-based file makes it far more easily accessible. An online system could also widen the accessibility of the tribunal process. It is envisaged that continuous online hearings will radically reduce the length of the appeals process in most cases, from an average of 20 weeks to one to two weeks. However, it is yet to be seen the extent

---

[46] For a discussion of administrative justice values, see Partington, Martin (1999) 'Restructuring administrative justice? The redress of citizens' grievances', *Current Legal Problems*, 53, 173; Tomlinson, Joe (2017) 'The grammar of administrative justice values', *Journal of Social Welfare and Family Law*, 39(4), 524–37.

[47] Prince, Sue (2019) '"Fine words butter no parsnips": Can the principle of open justice survive the introduction of an online court?', *Civil Justice Quarterly*, 38(1), 111.

to which appellants in jurisdictions such as SSCS and FtTIAC are able to effectively use such a platform. Another related issue is how video-link communication is implemented fairly.[48] Tribunals spend most of their time looking at evidence trying to establish facts. There is a widely held assumption that this task is best undertaken by hearing the evidence in person through an oral hearing.[49] This may be because other means of providing oral evidence may be inadequate and thereby risk unfairness for appellants or reduce the ability of the other parties to test such evidence. It could also be because the judicial task of collecting and evaluating facts – especially the credibility of a witness – will often depend not just on the content of the oral evidence, but also on non-verbal forms of communication, such as the way in which the evidence has been presented and the appellant's demeanour.[50] Alternatively, there are the ways in which live evidence at an oral hearing is subject to a degree of formality and supervision by the tribunal. The tribunal can control the procedure to ensure that there is no misuse of the judicial process. At the same time, video-link hearings have been used for some time in social security, immigration bail hearings and Upper Tribunal error of law hearings. Other jurisdictions, such as in the US and Canada, have made increasing use of video links for live evidence.[51] Furthermore, using video links in error of law hearings is relatively uncontroversial because the proceedings typically take the form of a dialogue or conversation between representatives and the judge, with the appellant making little, if any, active contribution. How video-link hearings can be

---

[48] For recent government testing on this, see Rossner, Meredith and McCurdy, Martha (2018) *Implementing Video hearings (Party-to-State): A Process Evaluation*, London: HM Courts & Tribunals Service.

[49] *Secretary of State for the Home Department v Nare (evidence by electronic means) Zimbabwe* [2011] UKUT 00443 (IAC), [17].

[50] *R (Mohibullah) v Secretary of State for the Home Department* [2016] UKUT 561 (IAC), [90].

[51] Federman (note 39 above); Eagly (note 39 above).

effective in tribunals that have an important fact-finding function presents a design challenge: the need to develop platforms where evidence can be given effectively and in a way that judges can have confidence in.

Fourth, and linked to the questions of the implementation of traditional values and effective communication between parties, there are multiple design questions concerning how fair procedures are ensured in online tribunals.[52] The online process promises huge changes in the tribunal process. This raises a host of questions. As noted above, one prominent example is the possible use of video-link technology in evidence-gathering. There is a range of questions about how these developments may be seen through the prism of the legal principles of procedural fairness, as well as how the use of technology may impact claimants' perceived sense of procedural justice.[53] Beyond what is legally considered to be procedurally fair, there is an important 'human element' in play here. The physical architecture of a courtroom, for example, can often condition people's experiences and perceptions of their treatment.[54] How online processes can be designed to maintain and maybe even enhance procedural fairness – both in the legal sense and the perception of appellants – presents varied design issues.

Fifth, there is the issue of how online processes – and surrounding systems – are designed to ensure appellants are not digitally excluded. While some appellants may find online processes more accessible, some groups are either unable or unwilling to use the internet for important issues such as a

---

[52] In legal terms, it is important to keep in mind the common law principles of procedural fairness and the right to a fair trial under Article 6 of the European Convention on Human Rights.

[53] For an example in a different context, see Wells, Helen (2008) 'The techno-fix versus the fair cop: Procedural (in)justice and automated speed limit enforcement', *The British Journal of Criminology*, 48(6), 798–817.

[54] Mulcahy, Linda (2010) *Legal Architecture: Justice, Due Process and the Place of Law*, Abingdon: Routledge.

tribunal case. Some people cannot afford internet access (or good internet access).[55] Some of those people may have access at a library or some other place, but their access – in terms of privacy, time and convenience – is likely to be less than those who have their own at-home connection. Beyond this, connection quality and coverage varies drastically across the UK.[56] Some people quite reasonably may not wish to have an important matter such as their entitlement to social security benefits or immigration determined online. The MoJ and HMCTS have recognised the need to support people who have difficulty using technology, particularly older people, children, people with disabilities, those without digital skills and those with poor literacy or English skills. In February 2017, the MoJ published its general approach to 'assisted digital' services. It promised support for people who have trouble with using technology: 'we will ensure that our assisted digital support takes into account the needs of those who are elderly or have disabilities, those with poor literacy or English skills, and those who lack access to technology because of cost or geography.'[57] The stated intention is to ensure that assisted digital services are designed to meet the needs of the end user of a digital service, mainly unrepresented appellants, litigants in person and professional users. An 'assisted digital' support programme is being developed to help those who need support to use online systems. There is a team within HMCTS investigating this issue and piloting new processes. This involves

---

[55] In 2015, of the 14% of households in Great Britain with no internet access, some explained this on the basis of equipment costs being too high (14%) and access costs being too high (12%); see ONS (Office for National Statistics) (2015) 'Statistical bulletin: Internet access – Households and individuals'.

[56] British Infrastructure Group (2016) *Broadband: A New Study into Broadband Investment and the Role of BT and Openreach.*

[57] Ministry of Justice (2017) *Transforming Our Justice System: Assisted Digital Strategy, Automatic Online Conviction and Statutory Standard Penalty, and Panel Composition in Tribunals: Government Response*, p 11.

government working with an independent, contracted-in supplier with the aim of providing a network of accessible assistance. It is expected that '[t]elephone and webchat services will also be available and clearly signposted for those who already have access to IT but require extra support, and paper channels will be maintained for those who need them.'[58] How appellants at risk of digital exclusion are managed appropriately and fairly, without undermining the wider purposes of digitalisation, will require appeal and assisted digital processes to be carefully designed.

Sixth, online appeals must be designed to fit into the wider administrative justice landscape. Administrative justice is both a fragmented and integrated landscape. It is comprised of a range of different systems (internal review, tribunals, judicial review) and different policy areas (social security, immigration, tax). Changes to one part of the wider landscape can have implications for another part. The introduction of digital tribunals prompts multiple questions in this respect. For instance, in the context of social security, there is a possibility that – next to an online tribunal procedure – MR looks obsolete. How will the two systems – one paper-based and the other online – work together? Good online tribunals designs would be sensitive to the wider administrative justice system in which they exist, such as processes like MR. There is plenty of room for creative improvements here too. It is widely argued that government should learn from tribunal decisions to improve initial decision-making.[59] The prospect of digitalisation presents the opportunity to build in better and quicker feedback loops that consume less time, effort and money.

Seventh, there is the question of data collection. Digital systems collect massive amounts of data. They can do this

---

[58] Ibid, p 27.

[59] See, generally, Thomas, Robert (2015) 'Administrative justice, better decisions, and organisational learning', *Public Law*, 111.

consciously through, for instance, asking for specific information on a form. But digital systems also create data through their operation (often in the form of metadata). Digitalising a tribunals system historically reliant on paper raises questions in relation to data collection and protection. From a research and system improvement perspective, there is a potential bounty here too: the collection of mass data that is easily searchable opens clear gateways for new research, at a much faster rate. What data is collected is a central question. So is what data will be published.

Finally, there is the need to design an efficient process. As noted at the outset of this chapter, efficiency is a key driver in the HMCTS reforms. Technology-based reforms tend to be based on the idea of frontloading investment and gaining long-term savings. That seems to be the case with *Transforming Our Justice System* too. At the same time, systems often work in unpredictable ways and contain hidden costs. If the value of efficiency is to be a key driver, we must understand what efficiencies are actually generated and at what cost to other values, such as access to justice. There is also a need to understand false efficiencies. In March 2016 Sir Ernest Ryder explained how Money Claims Online:

> … has been in operation since 2001 and has over 180,000 users annually. But once the "submit" button is pressed by the user or their representative, a civil servant at the other end has to print the e-form, and make up a paper file. From that point on, we are back to square one: almost back to the Dickensian model of justice via the quill pen.[60]

There are two major 'risks' in respect of efficiency. The first is that the online system makes appealing so easy that there is an upsurge in cases that cannot be easily handled. The second is

---

[60] Ryder, Ernest (2016) 'The Modernisation of Access to Justice in Times of Austerity', The Ryder Lecture, University of Bolton.

that the use of online systems will not be as broad as is predicted as there will be two systems – online and traditional – that inefficiently co-exist. This second 'risk' may lead to some appellants being pressed into using the online tribunal.

I have provided only a broad overview of some key issues that designing online tribunal processes presents, yet it is clear that the design challenges are many and varied. Digitalisation essentially requires us to examine the justice system we have at present and to recreate a new system on the basis of what we have learned so far. This is no easy task and is made more difficult by the fact that seemingly small details may have significant effects on how online tribunals operate in practice.

Recommendations

The introduction of online tribunal processes marks another key turning point in the long history of tribunals. Digitalisation also represents the latest in a number of significant changes to tribunals in just recent years. The introduction of online tribunals must be understood in the wider context of these changes. From that wider perspective, the introduction of online tribunals could lead to the continued marginalisation of the role of tribunals or go some way to making them more effective as an administrative justice process. The outcome of the government's gamble to get more for less by using technology in tribunals will only be seen once all of the reforms are completed – something that is expected within the next few years.

As there is little in the way of detailed evidence available as to how online tribunal appeals will work in practice, the most important recommendations that can be offered at this stage go to monitoring and design. The issues of design are addressed in more detail in the next chapter. As for monitoring of online appeals, at least two elements are critical. First, a coherent scheme of data collection on online appeals and assisted digital – which is in line with data ethics and privacy considerations

– must be developed. Furthermore, such data should be made publicly available for review by external stakeholders and researchers. Second, the government should not only conduct research for the development of online processes, but also pursue, commission and enable detailed empirical research that examines how online processes are working in practice – as part of a wider commitment to continued evaluation of new online systems. This will provide detailed insights into whether online appeals are proving effective or whether they have weakened administrative justice in the way some fear they might.

FOUR

How digital administrative justice is made

The recent MoJ and HMCTS digitalisation reforms, discussed in Chapter Three, have been developed primarily as an operational project. That is to say that, despite the reforms representing a major change to justice processes, there is expected to be comparatively little by way of substantive changes to the law (at least in the foreseeable future). The existing law will instead be given new practical enacting frameworks. This approach means that responsibility for deliberating on and developing digital processes has been left largely with civil servants within HMCTS and the MoJ, with Parliament only providing a 'drip-feed' of legislative activity and oversight thus far.[1] Other developments in the digitalisation of administrative justice – such as the increasing use of automated processes in public sector decision-making –

---

[1] Rozenberg, Joshua (2018) *The Online Court: Will IT Work?*, Guildford: Legal Education Foundation, p 12. The main legislative activity has focused on the Prison and Courts Bill, which has stalled on various occasions. So far we only have the Courts and Tribunals (Judiciary and Functions of Staff) Act 2018. See also House of Commons Committee of Public Accounts (2018) *Transforming Courts and Tribunals*, HC 976.

have seen similar patterns. At the core of the story of how digital technology is impacting administrative justice is therefore civil servants, their approach to process design and the government's own IT capabilities.[2]

One key trend in administrative justice design in UK central government is that it is increasingly influenced by 'agile' or 'design-thinking' approaches.[3] This method is underpinning how many online administrative justice systems, including online tribunals, are being constructed, and is being widely promoted by leading technologists in government. Although many lawyers will not be familiar with it, design thinking is now a well-established field of study in its own right. The premise is that design as a cognitive process – a 'more interpretative, intuitive mind-set that characterizes the arts and creative professions'[4] – does not have to focus on products alone but can be extended to other fields.[5] Design thinking therefore seeks to distil and find new applications for design as a way of thinking. Initially emerging in the 1960s and 1970s,[6] the idea of studying design as a mode of thought was developed in the 1980s through to the modern day.[7] There are long-established journals in the field, such as *Design Studies* and *Design Issues*. There are also many courses available that offer recognised training in this area, along with multiple research centres developing new lines of

---

[2] The key work on the design of administrative justice processes in the UK is Le Sueur, Andrew and Bondy, Varda (2012) *Designing Redress*, London: Public Law Project. There is limited literature directly addressing the issue.

[3] I use the two terms interchangeably for the purposes of the discussion here.

[4] Bason, Christian (2010) *Leading Public Sector Innovation: Co-creating for a Better Society*, Bristol: Policy Press, p 138.

[5] Simon, Herbert A. (1969) *The Sciences of the Artificial*, Cambridge, MA: MIT Press.

[6] Ibid.

[7] See, for example, Rowe, Peter G. (1987) *Design Thinking*, Cambridge, MA: MIT Press.

thought.[8] There is no precise definition of design thinking or the agile method.[9] However, the core of the approach appears to rest on emphasising the perspective of 'users' of systems, developing prototype systems and consistently testing systems with users.[10] These core tenets are commonly expressed in the five-part, non-linear design method of:

- empathising with users
- defining the problem
- ideating
- prototyping and
- testing.[11]

Within this framework, multiple tools to support each of these exercises have also been developed.[12] For instance, the use

---

[8]   For instance, Stanford University now hosts the Legal Design Lab, a leading centre. A range of other organisations is working in this space too, for example, NuLawLab, Legal Design Jam and Carnegie Mellon's CyLab Usable Privacy & Security Law. The growing literature on the application of design thinking to justice is well set out in Ursel, Susan (2017) 'Building better law: How design thinking can help us be better lawyers, meet new challenges, and create the future of law', *Windsor Yearbook of Access to Justice*, 34(1), 28.

[9]   Kimbell, Lucy (2012) 'Rethinking design thinking: Part 1', *Design and Culture*, 3(3), 285–306; Kimbell, Lucy (2012) 'Rethinking design thinking: Part II', *Design and Culture*, 4(2), 129–48. See also Dorst, Kees (2011) 'The core of "design thinking" and its application', *Design Studies*, 32(6), 521–32; Buchanan, Richard (1992) 'Wicked problems in design thinking', *Design Issues*, 8(2), 5–21.

[10]   Plattner, Hasso, Meinel, Christoph and Leifer, Larry (eds) (2011) *Design Thinking*, Berlin and Heidelberg: Springer-Verlag, pp 14–15.

[11]   These stages have been expressed in various ways; see, for example, Rowe (note 7 above); Simon (note 5 above); Hagan, Margaret (2017) *Law by Design* [E-book].

[12]   Alves, Rui and Nunes, Nuno Jardim (2013) 'Towards a Taxonomy of Service Design Methods and Tools', in João Falcão e Cunha, Mehdi Snene and Henrietta Sampaio da Nóvoa (eds) *Exploring Services Science*, IESS:

of 'journey-mapping' tools is now common. These tools help system-designers trying to understand how users come to use a service and what they experience at each step of the process. With the development of the agile approach, its influence has grown in many sectors – architecture, business, technology and management, to name only a few.[13] Law is now one of those sectors,[14] and so too is administration.[15] The agile approach

International Conference on Exploring Services Science, vol 143, Cham, Switzerland: Springer, pp 215–29.

[13] See, for example, Brooks Jr, Frederick P. (2010) *The Design of Design: Essays from a Computer Scientist*, Boston, MA: Addison Wesley; Martin, Roger L. (2009) *Design of Business: Why Design Thinking Is the Next Competitive Advantage*, Brighton, MA: Harvard Business School Press.

[14] Much thinking is taking place on the other side of the Atlantic in particular, see Hagan (note 11 above); Hagan, Margaret (2014) 'Design thinking and law: A perfect match', *Law Practice Today*, January; Rostain, Tanina, Skalbeck, Roger and Mulcahy, Kevin G. (2018) 'Thinking like a lawyer, designing like an architect: Preparing students for the 21st century practice', *Chicago-Kent Law Review*, 88(3), 743; Owen, Charles L., Staudt, Ronald W. and Pedwell, Edward B. (2001) *Access to Justice: Meeting the Needs of Selfrepresented Litigants*, Chicago, IL: Institute of Design and ChicagoKent College of Law, Illinois Institute of Technology; Szabo, Mark (2010) *Design Thinking in Legal Practice Management*, Boston, MA: Design Management Institute; Clarke, John A. and Borys, Bryan D. (2011) 'Usability is free: Improving efficiency by making the court more userfriendly', *Future Trends in State Courts*, 76; Mastarone, Ginnifer L. and Feinberg, Susan (2007) 'Access to Legal Services: Organizing Better Selfhelp Systems', Professional Communication Conference; Lippe, Paul (2013) 'Do lawyers have the "design mojo" needed to rethink the delivery of legal services?', *ABA Journal: Legal Rebels*, December; Ball, W. David (2014) 'Redesigning sentencing', *McGeorge Law Review*, 46, 817.

[15] See, for example, Clarke, Amanda and Craft, Jonathan (2018) 'The twin faces of public sector design', *Governance*, 32(1), 5–21; Clarke, Amanda and Craft, Jonathan (2017) 'The vestiges and vanguards of policy design in a digital context', *Canadian Public Administration*, 60(4), 476–97; Anthopoulos, Leo G., Siozos, Panagiotis and Tsoukalas, Ioannis A. (2007) 'Applying participatory design and collaboration in digital public services for discovering and redesigning eGovernment services', *Government Information Quarterly*, 24(2), 353–76. There has also been some interesting design

has now become widely influential in the UK civil service and is gradually replacing, at least partially, the traditional top-down (or 'waterfall') approaches of civil servants in a variety of important policy areas.[16] This is a key cultural change within central government that the digitalisation of administrative justice is simultaneously perpetuating and being shaped by. The most obvious manifestation of this trend to those outside of administration is how the language of governance is embracing a new vocabulary: 'digital by default', 'agile', 'open', 'innovation', 'platform'.[17] This is not meaningless bureaucratic language, but representative of important underlying changes of practice.

This chapter reflects on the increasing influence of agile processes in relation to the design of the administrative justice system. It starts by outlining the recent record of government IT projects, how agile methods were embraced as part of an attempt to avoid repeating historical failures, and what the main components of the approach are. I also draw on the limited evidence available to show how these approaches are being used in practice in the ongoing HMCTS tribunal reforms. I then turn to address how the 'politics' of agile are developing, ranging from the 'evangelicals', who believe the approach will herald a revolution in justice, to the 'anti-designers', who suggest that design processes involving technology may even pose threats

work in the context of the tax system; see Preston, Alan (2009) 'Designing the Australian Tax System', in Richard J. Boland and Fred Collopy (eds) *Managing as Designing*, Berkeley, CA: Stanford University Press; Terrey, Nina (2012) 'Managing by Design – A Case Study of the Australian Taxation Office', Unpublished PhD thesis, University of Canberra.

[16] Policy is also now part of the design movement. For an overview, see Bobrow, Davis B. (2006) 'Policy Design: Ubiquitous, Necessary, and Difficult', in B. Guy Peters and Jon Pierre (eds) *Handbook of Public Policy*, London: Sage Publications, pp 281–315; Bason (note 4 above). For a popular account of these ideas in the UK, see Hilton, Steve (2015) *More Human: Designing a World Where People Come First*, London: W.H. Allen & Co.

[17] O'Reilly, Tim (2011) 'Government as a platform', *Innovations*, 6(1), 13–40.

to key tenets of modern constitutionalism. After sketching out the emerging politics around agile, I show how its growth represents changing models of designing administrative justice. In particular, that it is attempting to shift emphasis on to users' preferences – something that I suggest ought to be welcomed but also potentially puts more traditional legal and good governance values in a precarious position. Finally, I look at the design of the agile process itself, making some recommendations on how it can potentially become more effective.

My overall argument is that, on the basis of the present evidence, the best hope for agile methods must be that they achieve the best systems within pre-established policy objectives and the practical realities of government. However, for the promised benefits of agile methods to be achieved, it must be applied with integrity. Moreover, greater thought must be given to how wider concerns and practice of public law and good administration fit alongside the agile method.

How agile developed and how it works

Historically, government has been a place where major IT projects faced almost certain disaster. The public sector has a long record of expensive failures and under-used services.[18] This has been a problem in many countries, but the UK has been described in such terms as 'ground zero for IT management failures'[19] and 'a world leader in ineffective IT schemes for government.'[20] IT failures within UK government have taken various forms: spiralling costs, delays and the collapse of proposed

---

[18] Dunleavy, Patrick, Margetts, Helen, Bastow, Simon and Tinkler, Jane (2008) *Digital Era Governance: IT Corporations, the State, and e-Government*, Oxford: Oxford University Press.

[19] Clarke, Amanda (2017) *Digital Government Units: Origins, Orthodoxy and Critical Considerations for Public Management Theory and Practice*, Working Paper, p 5.

[20] Dunleavy et al, p 70 (note 18 above).

reforms. The reasons for such failures have been multi-layered and complex.[21] Things have, however, changed in recent years. Against a backdrop of widespread condemnation of IT projects, growing expense, a global financial crisis and various reports,[22] the Government Digital Service was established. Introduced in 2011 as 'Alphagov', the Government Digital Service is a unit within the Cabinet Office with a mandate across the whole of government concerning digital strategy, services, hiring and procurement. Within a very short period of time, the Government Digital Service was widely seen as the global leader in digital government. It even topped the United Nations' E-government rankings.[23]

The Government Digital Service is seen as the first of a new breed of administrative organisations that have now spread across the world: government digital units.[24] Government digital units have certain distinctive features: they operate at the centre of the administration; they adopt a unified approach across government and borrow heavily from the tech sector in terms of their operational style; they introduce 'start-up' cultures associated with tech companies and prioritise user-centred design (adopting 'design-thinking' approaches); they exhibit a preference for data-driven decision-making; and they combine in-house talent with contracted-in talent to pursue government-led projects.[25] Government digital units typically also set down

---

[21] Clarke (note 19 above).

[22] House of Commons Public Administration Select Committee (2011) *Government and IT – 'A recipe for rip-offs': Time for a new approach*, HC 715-I; Lane-Fox, Martha (2010) *Directgov 2010 and Beyond: Revolution not Evolution* (www.gov.uk/government/publications/directgov-2010-and-beyond-revolution-not-evolution-a-report-by-martha-lane-fox).

[23] UN (United Nations) Department of Economic and Social Affairs (2016) *UN E-Government Survey 2016*.

[24] Similar configurations have been introduced in the US, Canada and Australia.

[25] Clarke (note 19 above).

criteria through service standard that all government digital services must comply with before they are put into action.

While government digital units are a growing trend internationally, they are still in their early days and there is limited research on them. Some questions also arise about their performance. Such units are not necessarily an all-conquering solution. In practice, these units have, perhaps quite naturally, sought to tackle 'low hanging fruit' first, fixing easy problems and making easy gains. This would, of course, make it easier to build an overall successful portfolio and make claims for further investment etc. More complex tasks – concerning, for example, large-scale organisational reforms such as the ongoing HMCTS reforms – may prove more difficult. The National Audit Office has noted that 'while many government services are now available online ... departments and [the Government Digital Service] have struggled to manage more complicated programmes and to improve the complex systems and processes that support public services.'[26] However, the Government Digital Service has reported that 12 of the 25 projects on its initial work programme will see the benefits outweigh the costs of development within 10 years. It has been further observed that there is a real possibility of resistance to government digital units from within administration itself. There are many reports of UK civil servants disliking the 'invasion' of the Government Digital Service. The following quote, from a former Cabinet Office employee in 2012, demonstrates vividly this sentiment:

I think the interesting thing is if you talk to civil servants who aren't kind of "GDSonites" then they say "oh GDS is such arrogant wankers coming in and telling us how to do our jobs." I mean I'm sure you've come across – I'm sure you've experienced the reputation of GDS within

---

[26] National Audit Office (2017) *Digital Transformation in Government*, p 7.

Whitehall, as you know not entirely positive. You know they are seen to be arrogant.[27]

Such internal dynamics can lead to difficulties, the possibility of resistance to digitalisation and the need for outreach work within government. The Government Digital Service is actively seeking to combat this perception via outreach initiatives, for example, explaining its role to civil servants through a Digital Academy. More importantly, government digital units may also raise serious accountability questions. As the technology revolution continues to take hold, provision and control of government digital services and infrastructure will become increasingly important. With the digital unit model, it has been suggested that 'the lines of accountability linking political decision-makers to government programming and spending [have] become blurred', and that this challenge is 'particularly acute in Westminster systems, with their vertical lines of individual ministerial accountability.'[28] On top of all of this, government digital units require sustained political support and can be very expensive.

Despite it still being early days in their development, it is apparent that the rise of government digital units is effectively creating what Amanda Clarke has dubbed a 'new government-IT orthodoxy'.[29] Certain key features define this shift. First, a preference for 'agile' user-centric development, with heavy use of prototyping. Second, changes in procurement methods, including more reliance on in-house talent and more use of (when outsourcing is used) small and medium-sized enterprises. Third, the use of 'open' standards that allow solutions to be shared and reused across government (the Government Digital Service describes this approach as one that aggregates demand across government for common services but disaggregates the

---

[27] Clarke, p 32 (note 19 above).

[28] Ibid, p 36.

[29] Ibid, p 15.

supply of these services). Fourth, the creation of government-wide policies on digital initiatives. And fifth, the building of a new culture around digital service.

One core aspect of this 'new orthodoxy' of technology in government is the growing use of agile design processes. The agile approach is now routinely found in any aspect of government where the Government Digital Service has been involved. In the context of the HMCTS reforms discussed in Chapter Three, the Government Digital Service has been very influential and the agile approach has been widely adopted in order to implement those changes. HMCTS' specific model has the following four stages:

1. *Discovery:* Finding out what users need, what to measure and what the constraints are.
2. *Alpha:* Building a prototype, testing it with users and learning about it.
3. *Beta:* Scaling up and going public.
4. *Live:* Learning how continuously to improve the live service.

This approach has also been adopted alongside the 'Digital Service Standard', which the Government Digital Service states that 'all public facing transactional services must meet.'[30] This Standard includes requirements to 'understand user needs', 'do ongoing user research', 'use agile methods' and 'iterate and improve frequently'. HMCTS has also adopted new tools – such as journey and stakeholder mapping – that are traditionally part of the agile approach. These new agile approaches – manifesting how 'digital-era policy design instruments tend to privilege the participation of non-government actors in government

---

[30] Gov.uk (no date) 'Digital Service Standard' (www.gov.uk/service-manual/service-standard). A design manual is also available, which includes processes for system design and testing.

activities'[31] through what are commonly called 'co-production' techniques[32] – have synchronised easily with the increasing emphasis placed on the 'user perspective' in administrative justice policy in recent decades.[33]

Aside from the Government Digital Service, Policy Lab – a small team within the Cabinet Office established in 2014 – has also made a concerted effort to promote agile methods within government. Policy Lab was created as part of wider changes to the Civil Service.[34] In response to challenges from politicians, academia, the press and others, the *Civil Service Reform Plan* was made in 2012. It made a commitment to make 'open policy-making' the default approach. This meant that policy-making should draw on a full range of external experts, from academics to those who will deliver the policy. It was also promised that civil servants working on policy will have the necessary skills and expertise, can use up-to-date tools and techniques, and have a clear understanding of what works in practice.[35] One

---

[31] Clarke and Craft (2017), p 482 (note 15 above).

[32] Joshi, Anuradha and Moore, Mick (2004) 'Institutionalised co-production: Unorthodox public service delivery in challenging environments', *Journal of Development Studies*, 40(4), 31–49. See also Bovaird, Tony and Loeffler, Elke (2013) *We're All in this Together: Harnessing User and Community Co-Production of Public Outcomes*, Birmingham: Institute of Local Government Studies, University of Birmingham.

[33] For some background discussion on the rise of user-centred design in administrative justice policy, see Tomlinson, Joe (2017) 'The grammar of administrative justice values', *Journal of Social Welfare and Family Law*, 39(4), 524–37.

[34] For background on the creation of Policy Lab, see Kimbell, Lucy (2015) *Applying Design Approaches to Policy Making: Discovering Policy Lab*, Brighton: University of Brighton; Bailey, Jocelyn and Lloyd, Peter (2016) 'The Introduction of Design to Policymaking: Policy Lab and the UK Government', Design Research Society 50th Anniversary Conference. For a wider discussion on the development of this type of organisation, see Bellafontaine, Teresa (2013) *Innovation Labs: Bridging Think Tanks and Do Tanks*, Policy Horizons Canada.

[35] HM Government (2012) *Civil Service Reform Plan*, June.

year later, a Civil Service report promised to fund a Policy Lab to promote innovative techniques such as design thinking to approach policy problems in a new way.[36] It also promised to develop a culture where there was openness to new evidence, which would involve a broader range of experts and processes where practical experimentation would be the starting point for solving problems. This means that developing process designs by trialling, testing and iterating was widely encouraged. The ongoing remit of Policy Lab is to support policy-makers to change their approach to policy-making by demonstrating new tools and techniques, offering skills training and facilitating long-term shifts in policy-making practice.[37] Policy Lab works with a range of partners within government and sees its work as pushing for design-led change within the policy-making community in government.[38]

It is unclear exactly how agile processes have been working in practice, especially in the context of the HMCTS reforms to courts and tribunals.[39] Indeed, further research into the dynamics of these processes would be very insightful in terms of both understanding the process – what its benefits and limitations are – and how its operation may be improved in the context of administrative justice going forwards. The most information, in the context of the HMCTS reforms, is known about the agile method as it is being applied in the context of putting the social security tribunal on a digital footing. A summary released by government gives an impression of the scale and nature of this exercise.[40] From June 2017 to October 2018, the team focusing

---

[36] Civil Service (2013) *Twelve Actions to Professionalise Policy Making: A Report by the Policy Profession Board*, October.

[37] Kimbell, p 5 (note 34 above).

[38] Ibid.

[39] The best resource for this has been the Inside HMCTS Blog, https://insidehmcts.blog.gov.uk

[40] These numbers are based on the most charitable reading of the data published under FOIA Request No 180918020.

on the tribunal conducted seven rounds of 'discovery' research and eight rounds of 'alpha' testing. The testing was done with a variety of users: appellants, judges, senior medical members of the tribunals, claimant representatives and the DWP. For the testing, the total number of users engaged by the time the data was produced was 68; 29 were appellants and 26 were judges, along with two expert medical members of tribunals. From the DWP, five officials and five presenting officers were involved. One representative was spoken to. Most of the 'lab' testing sessions were done in London (13), with other labs being held in Manchester (1), Birmingham (1) and Newcastle (1). One session was held remotely. Around this, a series of more traditional research projects – such as surveys – were undertaken, but little is known about those exercises. What this information suggests is that the testing activities within the agile process being used in the HMCTS reform programme are, in practice, on a relatively small scale. There may be more activities occurring now, but the general opaqueness of agile processes makes this impossible to establish at present.

Beyond waterfall: changing models of design

How can we understand the shift in approach that is occurring in administrative justice design processes? The key change appears to be one of emphasis, from professional (civil servant) judgement to user judgement.[41] In other words, the traditional 'waterfall' model of design is being rejected where agile methods are adopted, at least partially.[42] Instead of system designs originating within the administration based on internal

---

[41] On the emphasis of users generally, see Mintrom, Michael and Luetjens, Joannah (2016) 'Design thinking in policymaking processes: Opportunities and challenges', *Australian Journal of Public Administration*, 75(3), 391.

[42] How design approaches link in with traditional approaches remains an unresolved question.

views on what operational demands are, the new model of design seeks to have civil servants relinquish some degree of control via prioritising user preferences. These preferences are understood through the activities of prototyping, testing and research. From one perspective, this involves opening up what used to be a relatively closed policy discussion about system design to involve users. This is part of a wider trend in public administration towards user participation in the design process – other methods, aside from agile design, have also been used to achieve similar ends. For instance, many administrations are trialling the crowdsourcing of policy with the aim of increasing participation and finding better results.[43] This shift in orientation is also represented in how theories of public administration in the emerging digital era have moved from traditional Weberian ideas of structured bureaucracy[44] to emphasising non-governmental actors being part of a more open process of designing the state.[45]

In seeking to change the nature of the conversation to be more open, what preferences are most prominent in the conversation may also change. Under the old model, the

---

[43] See, for example, Aitamurto, Tanja and Landemore, Helene (2015) 'Five design principles for crowdsourced policymaking: Assessing the case of crowdsourced off-road traffic law in Finland', *Journal of Social Media for Organizations*, 2(1), 1–19; Gao, Huji, Wang, Xufei, Barbier, Geoffrey and Liu, Huan (2011) 'Promoting Coordination for Disaster Relief – From Crowdsourcing to Coordination', in John Salerno, Shanchieh Jay Yang, Dana Nau and Sun-Ki Chai (eds) *Social Computing, Behavioural-Cultural Modelling, and Prediction*, Berlin and Heidelberg: Springer, 197–204.

[44] Weber, Max (1922) *Economy and Society*, Chapter 11.

[45] Dunleavy et al (note 18 above); Noveck, Beth Simone (2009) *Wiki Government: How Technology Can Make Government Better*, Washington, DC: Brookings Institute Press; O'Reilly (note 17 above); Dunleavy, Patrick and Hood, Christopher (1994) 'From old public administration to new public management', *Public Money & Management*, 14(3), 9–16; Pollitt, Christopher and Bouckaert, Geert (2011) *Public Management Reform: A Comparative Analysis: New Public Management, Governance, and the Neo-Weberian State*, Oxford: Oxford University Press.

priorities as determined by policy officials were central. Broadly speaking, these were often understood to be concerns of system-manageability (for example, cost and speed of processing) and classical values of good governance (for example, procedural fairness, independence). User needs may have also been factored in to the process but traditionally, this would be done based on working out what a rational user would require. By including users more directly in the conversation about the design of systems, other preferences may gain more traction. For instance, considerations such as convenience and speed – often understood to be key preferences of users – may be given much more emphasis if user input is taken into account seriously.[46]

It is important to note, however, that the agile design model does not actually pass decision-making control to users, as that remains with government. The impact of widening the conversation is dependent on how views are factored in overall by officials. Moreover, when agile methods and processes are adopted, they are used within the limits of the relevant department's budget (which is usually fixed in advance) and broadly pre-established policy objectives. This means that the conversation that is opened up is typically narrow; for instance, it is about *how* a system or part of a system operates online rather than *if* a system operates online.

An emerging politics of design?

Agile methodologies have, as noted above, been adopted across various sectors. Given this rapid growth, it is perhaps unsurprising that a politics around the use of agile design methodologies is now starting to emerge. A range of positions

---

[46] Berthoud, Richard and Bryson, Alex (1997) 'Social security appeals: What do the claimants want?', *Journal of Social Security Law*, 4(1), 17–41; Richardson, Genevra and Genn, Hazel (2007) 'Tribunals in transition', *Public Law*, 116.

can be taken, in particular in relation to governments' use of this approach, running from the more to the less enthusiastic. It is helpful to categorise views into four commonly held viewpoints.[47]

First, there are those who may be labelled *the evangelicals*. These are people who suggest that agile methodologies are waiting to revolutionise the administrative justice system, and the rest of the world needs to catch up. There are many international conferences on agile methodologies and legal design. These are often not forums primarily for critical reflection of the approach itself, but more for discussion on how the approach can be advanced, applied and promoted. For advocates of this approach, it could even be suggested that democratic participation is enhanced through agile processes, as individuals have a greater role in the process of designing government.[48]

Second, there are the *moderate advocates*. These are those who promote design thinking as an idea but also seek to question its application and how it integrates into extant ways of thinking about administrative justice. Canadian administrative law scholar Lorne Sossin is a good example of a moderate advocate. In a recent article, he stated his belief that 'design frameworks will transform how we think about administrative justice.'[49] His claim was that design thinking, and in particular, user-centred design, has been 'too often is missing in the design of administrative tribunals.'[50] Instead, he suggests, when lawyers have focused on design they have focused on design in a narrow legal sense,

---

[47] These are generally broad characterisations of different viewpoints.

[48] For a discussion on this point, see O'Reilly (note 17 above); Noveck (note 45 above); Margetts, Helen and Dunleavy, Patrick (2013) 'The second wave of digital-era governance: A quasi-paradigm for government on the Web', *Philosophical Transactions of the Royal Society A: Mathematical, Physical and Engineering Sciences*, 371.

[49] Sossin, Lorne (2017) 'Designing administrative justice', *Windsor Yearbook of Access to Justice*, 34(1), 87–111.

[50] Ibid, p 87.

such as the design of statutory mandates and procedures.[51] At the same time, in government, a 'top-down' policy-making process that serves the interests of a ruling government has been adopted.[52] The result, Sossin claims, is that the 'administrative justice system in Canada at all levels of Government (federal, provincial, municipal, Indigenous) is generally fragmented, poorly coordinated, under-resourced in relation to the needs of its users and has multiple barriers of entry.'[53] His view is that the application of design thinking, with its 'bottom-up' philosophy, will lead to overall better systems. Sossin, however, acknowledges that many tenets of the design-thinking approach that he outlines have long been promoted, by academics and by others.[54] He takes the position that agile methods are an evolution of an existing and helpful approach, the application of which needs to be expanded.

Third, there are the *sceptics,* who are uncertain what the agile approach adds to existing ways of thinking about designing administrative justice systems. The concern here is that the adoption of agile methods may represent no more than superficial language that dresses up the process of administrative justice reform in bureaucratic language, potentially even obfuscating important issues of substantive policy and process design as a result.

Finally, and this is perhaps the most interesting of categories, there appears to be an emerging school of *anti-designers.* A

---

[51] Ibid, p 87. For instance, Sossin cites from the Canadian context: Ellis, Ron (1987) 'Administrative tribunal design', *Canadian Journal of Administrative Law & Practice*, 1, 134; Ellis, Ron (2013) *Unjust by Design: Canada's Administrative Justice System*, Vancouver, BC: University of British Columbia Press.

[52] Ibid.

[53] Ibid.

[54] See, for example, Leggatt, Andrew (2001) *Tribunals for Users: One System, One Service, Report of the Review of Tribunals*, London: Ministry of Justice, paras 15.16–15.17.

clear articulation of this type of stance, albeit made in the context of regulation, has been offered by Deirdre Mulligan and Kenneth Bamberger, two US scholars who launched a critique of 'governance by design'.[55] They argue that design approaches 'bake in' certain types of political preference, and that conventional structures of accountability are 'fundamentally ill-equipped' to provide effective scrutiny of this. The risk they identify is that design approaches may subvert traditional models of public governance.[56] They argue that 'governance-by-design has undermined important governance norms' and its form, coupled with the lack of space for scrutiny, means there has rarely been 'a meta-discussion about when and whether it is appropriate to enlist technology in the service of values at all.'[57] The result may be that the outcome of a design process is that key choices 'recede from the political as they become what "is" rather than what [democratic] politics has determined ought to be.'[58]

Agile as institutional design

Thinking about the 'design of design' may seem odd, but it is important. The process by which systems are created are naturally vital to the system citizens ultimately experience. It is important therefore to consider the positive and negative features of any design process.

At the outset, it ought to be noted that agile approaches have some features that may be considered helpful. First, they can lower the risk of large-scale disasters. Building systems piece by

---

[55] Mulligan, Deirdre K. and Bamberger, Kenneth A. (2018) 'Saving governance-by-design', *California Law Review*, 106(3), 697–784. The argument in this article has a wider scope than just agile processes, but it engages with similar concerns about 'design' method in the context of government technology.

[56] Ibid.

[57] Ibid, p 698.

[58] Ibid.

piece can mean that problems can be more easily located and fixed than in one large system. It also avoids the moment where there is one 'big-bang' roll-out of a new process (which carries the potential for huge disaster). This is because, under the agile method, new processes incrementally go online after rounds of testing. Agile may also more easily facilitate feedback to allow for improvement beyond the initial design phase.[59] Second, agile methods can give users of the system a greater voice in the design process. It has often been observed that administrative justice processes have been influenced by elite users of the system – particularly lawyers – rather than ordinary citizens.[60] At the same time, agile processes can also allow the actual voices of users to be heard, rather than assumptions being made about what users want or how they experience processes. Finally, agile processes seek to foster a greater emphasis on evidence-based policy-making. This has long been argued to be necessary by administrative justice commentators.[61] With the growth of digital processes, there is also the possibility of capturing more detailed data on administrative justice processes (although there are debates around what data precisely should be collected, what data should be made public and what data should be shared across government). Agile processes may allow the most to be made of 'big data' through directly incorporating searching for all available evidence into the process.

Agile processes have various features, however, which may limit their effectiveness. There are two main types of limitation. First, there are those limitations that are intrinsic to the method itself. For instance, the iterative aspect of the agile method means that when research and testing is conducted, it is usually

---

[59] For a wider discussion of the role of this kind of feedback, see Coleman, Stephen and Gotz, John (2001) *Bowling Together: Online Public Engagement in Policy Deliberation*, London: Hansard Society.

[60] See, for example, Sossin (note 49 above).

[61] For a recent example, see UK Administrative Justice Institute (2018) *Research Roadmap*.

on specific parts of a process. Due to this, there remains a need for changes to be assessed in the wider systems in which they exist, as well as end-to-end testing of the overall processes that are built. Moreover, working in an iterative way can make it difficult for external stakeholders, including external researchers, experts and those affected by changes, to engage with the design process. Agile processes also put emphasis on what users want. As explained above, there may be many good reasons for installing processes that turn the dial in this direction. However, there is a risk with the present procedure of over-reliance on the user perspective, and care must be taken not to too willingly emphasise values often preferred by users – such as convenience – over traditional concerns such as procedural fairness.[62] With technologists and civil servants exercising a large amount of control over the important details of the design of systems, the importance of classical legal values, such as fair process, may get lost. Lord Reed, in the landmark *UNISON* ruling, gave a warning to this effect:

> … [t]he importance of the rule of law is not always understood. Indications of a lack of understanding include the assumption that the administration of justice is merely a public service like any other, that courts and tribunals are providers of services to the "users" who appear before them, and that the provision of those services is of value only to the users themselves and to those who are remunerated for their participation in the proceedings.'[63]

Agile design risks justice processes being conceived as 'merely a public service like any other.'

The financial costs of user research and testing may prove a further limitation. For example, to do effective user research,

---

[62] Berthoud and Bryson (note 46 above); Richardson and Genn (note 46 above).
[63] *R (UNISON) v Lord Chancellor* [2017] UKSC 51 [66].

research teams, that take relatively long periods of time to work, are required. The reliance on engaging with users could also present problems in some contexts. Tracking down users of the justice system willing to spend time talking with government about their experiences with government may pose problems. Some may be worried about engaging and others may not want to engage at all. It may even be difficult to find users in the first place. For instance, in respect of immigration tribunals, users may speak different languages, many have left the country and many may be cautious about disclosing information to government based on past negative experiences. The issues around the practical implementation, financial and otherwise, of the agile method may ultimately lead to user research and testing only being conducted on a small scale. This could undermine how representative, and therefore reliable, the outcomes of agile processes are. At the same time, this can give the impression that it provides 'more heat than fire with rhetoric far outpacing its uptake.'[64]

It must also be highlighted that agile testing is not public and focuses on narrow topics. It cannot therefore be seen as a proxy for deliberative, public debate or even traditional forms of public consultation. The relationship between traditional forms of public consultation and agile testing presents various tensions. In the current HMCTS reforms this tension is perhaps best demonstrated by how observers are complaining about a lack of consultation whereas the government feels as though it has been constantly consulting. This ultimately goes to a wider issue of how 'the role of individual citizens and non-governmental

---

[64] Clarke and Craft (2017) (note 15 above). See also Clarke, Amanda (2014) *Government-Citizen Relations on the Social Web: Canada and the United Kingdom*, Oxford: Oxford University Press; Clarke, Amanda and Francoli, Mary (2017) 'Digital Government and Permanent Campaigning', in Alex Marland, Anna Lennox Esselment and Thierry Giasson (eds) *Permanent Campaigning in Canada*, Vancouver, BC: University of British Columbia Press, 241–58.

organizations in social problem solving [by government] remains unclear in the digital age.'[65]

Finally, there are questions about the capacity of governments to move from traditional modes of working to new agile processes. Some studies have suggested this may be a key problem,[66] particularly in relation to the capacity of government to understand how to integrate new forms of evidence gathered by more citizen participation and big data.[67]

A second set of limitations relates to the application of agile methods in the wider context of political and governmental reality.[68] In this wider setting, agile methods are typically deployed within broadly pre-established policy objectives, meaning the results of the process, no matter how well-managed the method is, will also been limited. Governments may choose to reform a process for a number of reasons, and these motivating reasons often shape the overall process.[69] Perhaps most significantly, since agile processes have become more prevalent in the UK, they have usually been deployed within certain budget structures in mind, specifically, with the need to reduce costs or to ensure effective working within restricted budgets. If resources are scarce, there is simply going to be a limit to what is possible.

---

[65] Clarke and Craft (2017), p 484 (note 15 above).

[66] Mergel, Ines and Desouza, Kevin C. (2013) 'Implementing open innovation in the public sector: The case of challenge.gov', *Public Administration Review*, 73(6), 882–90; Clarke, Amanda (2019) *Opening the Government of Canada: The Federal Bureaucracy in the Digital Age*, Vancouver, BC: University of British Columbia Press.

[67] Painter, Martin and Pierre, Jon (2005) 'Unpacking Policy Capacity: Issues and Themes', in M. Painter and J. Pierre (eds) *Challenges to State Policy Capacity: Global Trends and Comparative Perspectives*, Basingstoke: Palgrave Macmillan, pp 1–18.

[68] Clarke and Craft (2017) (note 15 above). For further discussion, see Considine, Mark (2012) 'Thinking outside the box? Applying design theory to public policy', *Politics & Policy*, 40(4), 704–24.

[69] Le Sueur and Bondy (note 2 above). There is very limited literature directly addressing the issue.

The highest aim, therefore, can only be that agile methods have features that allow for the development of the best process within the money that is available. There also remains an old problem: the operational gap between government departments.[70] This wider institutional issue within central government can risk undermining drastically the benefit of agile approaches. There is little sense, for example, in HMCTS designing a user-friendly online social security tribunal procedure which is preceded by processes in the DWP that are often seen to be not user-friendly at all.[71] Calls for 'joined-up' thinking in administrative justice are nothing new. However, the lack of coordination between different government departments can undermine the deployment of the user-centred agile approach. Finally, there are obvious questions about how comfortably evidence fits alongside the more expressly political dynamics within administration.[72]

Recommendations

It is as axiomatic as anything is in administrative justice that making systems better for users is a good idea. The tricky questions relate to how that happens and the extent to which user preferences should be given priority. For the benefits of agile, as promised by it advocates, to be realised, the approach must be applied with integrity. Practically, the realities of government – with, for example, tight budgets and departmental

---

[70] Freedland, Mark (1999) 'The Crown and the Changing Nature of Government', in Maurice Sunkin and Sebastian Payne (eds) *The Nature of the Crown: A Legal and Political Analysis*, Oxford: Oxford University Press, Chapter 5.

[71] See, for example, Thomas, Robert and Tomlinson, Joe (2019: forthcoming) 'A different tale of judicial power: Administrative review as a problematic response to the judicialisation of tribunals', *Public Law*, which shows the effects the DWP's MR pre-appeal process has on the operation of the tribunal.

[72] Cairney, Paul (2016) *The Politics of Evidence-based Policy Making*, Basingstoke: Palgrave Macmillan.

silos – make this tricky. Furthermore, the limitations of the method – even when applied with integrity – must be accepted. Agile methods are typically deployed within broadly pre-established policy objectives, meaning the results of the process, no matter how well executed, will also be so limited. As such, it is difficult for agile methods to be thought of as a substitute for genuine public debate and consultation.

The best hope for agile methods must be that they achieve the best systems within pre-established policy objectives and the practical realties of government. Time will tell if this is the case in practice, and further investigation into the dynamics of these processes would be insightful, in terms of both developing understanding and improving the process. However, for now, various steps could be taken to improve the present design process. In particular, thought could be given to how wider concerns of ethics and good governance fit within the agile method, as well as allowing wider external engagement with the process. In this respect, a series of relatively low-cost improvements are possible. First, the fragmented nature of agile methods means that, even within the parameters of a particular design process, there may be a lack of joined-up thinking. Adopting end-to-end testing of processes at various stages could mitigate this risk. Second, to ensure traditional concerns of public law and good government – such as procedural fairness – are fully considered and not displaced inappropriately by user preferences, consideration should be given to setting up expert advisory groups on particular projects or to creating a good governance standard, to sit alongside the Government Digital Service's Service Standard. The aim would be to promote wider considerations than the agile method may directly facilitate. And third, to allow more external engagement with design processes, a commitment could be made that research undertaken within government as part of a design process – wherever practicable and within the appropriate limits of data protection laws, research ethics etc – will be published, even if only in summary form.[73] This could improve transparency and facilitate a wider public conversation.

---

[73] Instructive discussion and helpful principles can be found in Sedley, Sir Stephen (2016) *Missing Evidence: An Inquiry into the Delayed Publication of Government Commissioned Research*, Sense About Science.

FIVE

Conclusion

Digitalisation in the context of the administrative justice system presents a wide variety of issues. The case studies in this book have demonstrated that. It is essential that the ongoing incursion of digital technology into administrative justice is not seen as some distinct field of interest and activity, but as part of the core business of those concerned with public law and administrative justice. There will be no satisfying overall answer or theory that can be developed in response to this incursion. In administrative justice, generalisations are often unhelpful and rarely true. Different instances of digitalisation – whether they are imposed as part of public service provision or arise organically from technological innovation – need to be considered in their particular institutional and political contexts.

Given this, this book has sought to provide a framework for analysing unfolding developments in the digitalisation of administrative justice, and not an overarching prescriptive theory. It has argued that analysis must reflect on how developments with digital technology fit into the central and long-stranding administrative justice concerns of evidence, politics, models and design. It has highlighted the urgent need to study closely the empirical consequences of technology and revisit, and maybe even abandon, existing frameworks for understanding how administrative justice operates. By outlining this path forwards, I am essentially re-stating what Richard B. Stewart wrote at the end of his famous 1975 essay, 'The reformation of American administrative law', considering the role of administrative law in the context of a changing US state and polity: '[g]iven "the undefined foreboding of something unknown," we can know only that we must spurn superficial analysis and simplistic remedies, girding ourselves to shoulder, for the indefinite future, the intellectual and social burdens of a dense complexity.'[1]

At the conclusion of writing this book, the growing digitalisation of administrative justice was forming a subtle backdrop for headlines. A report published by the UN Special Rapporteur on Extreme Poverty and Human Rights, Professor Philip Alston, castigated the UK's approach to welfare provision.[2] A key part of his findings related to the use of new technologies in administration. Professor Alston noted how '[g]overnment is increasingly automating itself with the use of data and new technology tools, including AI. Evidence shows that the human rights of the poorest and most vulnerable are especially at risk in such contexts.'[3] Among complaints of a lack of transparency and concerns about legal frameworks concerning data, Professor Alston saw fit to remind the government that: 'there is nothing inherent in Artificial Intelligence and other technologies that enable automation that threatens human rights and the rule of

---

[1] Stewart, Richard B. (1975) 'The reformation of American administrative law', *Harvard Law Review*, 88(8), 1667, p 1813. Citing Hegel, Georg (1949) *The Phenomenology of Mind* (2nd edn, translated by J. Baillie), Mineola, NY: Dover Publications, p 75.

[2] UN OHCHR (United Nations Office of the High Commissioner, Human Rights) (2018) 'Statement on Visit to the United Kingdom', by Professor Philip Alston, United Nations Special Rapporteur on extreme poverty and human rights, 16 November (www.ohchr.org/EN/NewsEvents/Pages/DisplayNews.aspx?NewsID=23881&LangID=E).

[3] Ibid.

law. The reality is that governments simply seek to operationalize their political preferences through technology; the outcomes may be good or bad.'[4]

The team at the DWP, while busy disputing the Special Rapporteur's findings, were also dealing with a ministerial transition.[5] The Minister for Work and Pensions in post during the week of Professor Alston's visit to the UK, Esther McVey MP, had resigned from the Cabinet in protest over the handling of Brexit negotiations. Brexit itself will represent another step towards reliance on digital administration in the UK. Given the amount of administrative change required in a small amount of time, it is hardly surprising that technology is being relied upon to manage the transition.[6] One major example is the EU Settlement Scheme, which has been established to enable EU citizens and their family members, currently residing within the UK, to apply for settled status following the UK's expected withdrawal from the EU.[7] To apply, applicants must complete an online application.[8] As part of this process, individuals must demonstrate a continuous period of residency within the UK, where they have not been absent from the country for more than 6 months within any 12-month period.[9] To confirm and

---

[4] Ibid.

[5] See, for example, Walker, Peter (2018) 'Amber Rudd condemns UN poverty report in combative return to frontline politics', *The Guardian*, 19 November (www.theguardian.com/politics/2018/nov/19/amber-rudd-un-poverty-report-return-frontline-politics).

[6] See, generally, Tomlinson, Joe and Lovdahl Gormsen, Liza (2018) 'Stumbling towards the UK's new administrative settlement: A study of competition law enforcement after Brexit', *Cambridge Yearbook of European Legal Studies*, 20, 233–51.

[7] Home Office (2018) *EU Settlement Scheme: EU Citizens and Their Family Members*, 1 November (https://assets.publishing.service.gov.uk/government/uploads/system/uploads/attachment_data/file/753971/eu-settlement-scheme-pb2-v1.0-ext.pdf).

[8] Ibid.

[9] Ibid, p 39.

establish this period of residency, the Home Office are deploying automated checks that engage tax and welfare databases and systems.[10] Where it has been algorithmically determined that an applicant has not met the requirements, they must then provide evidence to the contrary. These recent developments only reiterate further the urgency of analysing what digital technology means for administrative justice. My hope is that the discussion in this book has brought attention to, and provided a framework to understand and analyse, the wide variety of important challenges presented by ensuring justice in an increasingly digital state.

---

[10] Ibid, pp 41, 50.

Index

Page references for notes are followed by the note number